John Arne
RIISE

RUNNING MAN

John Arne
RIISE

RUNNING MAN

IN COLLABORATION WITH
Jens M. Johansson

TRANSLATED FROM THE NORWEGIAN BY
Paul Russell Garrett

The author has received support from
The Norwegian Non-fiction Literary Fund.

First published as a hardback by deCoubertin Books Ltd in 2018.

First Edition.

deCoubertin Books, 46B Jamaica Street, Baltic Triangle, Liverpool, L1 0AF.

www.decoubertin.co.uk

ISBN: 978-1-909245-69-3

A CIP catalogue record for this book is available from the British Library.
Translation by Paul Russell Garrett.
Cover design by Thomas Regan/Milkyone.
Typeset by Leslie Priestley.
Printed and bound by Jellyfish.

The author has received support from The Norwegian Non-fiction Literary Fund.

Prologue

'Should we start again?'

'Is it recording?'

'Yes.'

'What was the question?'

'Whether you realise that not everyone likes you'

'I get that. Sure.'

'How's that?'

'There are plenty of times when I haven't much liked myself either.'

'You're laughing?'

'Yes, but it's because this is something I'd rather not talk about.'

'What, that you don't always like yourself?'

'I don't know. I suppose I'm okay with that to a point. I suppose most people feel that way. We don't always behave the way we want to. No, there's something else that's far worse to consider. It's the fact that, after all, I know the circumstances surrounding everything that has happened. Imagine all the people who only know the version that has been told so far. What must they think of me?'

'What do you think they think?'

'If all I knew was that version, then I wouldn't have liked myself one bit. Who likes that guy?'

'...'

'Can't we talk about something different? Can't we start somewhere else?'

1

THE SOUND OF STUDS HITTING THE FLOOR IN THE PLAYERS' TUNNEL.
AC Milan have humiliated us in the first half. They're ahead by a score of 3–0.
We tumble into the dressing room. Nobody says a thing. I find my spot, slump down.
The final of the Champions League, 25 May 2005. The whole world is watching us,
and we've made a fool of ourselves. Sure, Milan have been on us like tigers, but
above all else we've made a fool of ourselves. The most important match of our lives
and we've been completely outplayed. I can hear the singing on the terraces outside,
through the concrete of the Atatürk Stadium in Istanbul. Our travelling supporters
are singing 'You'll Never Walk Alone'. It's an act of defiance, an impressive show of
solidarity. The stadium is no more than three years old, everything around us in the
dressing room is new, but we are worn out and broken.

Rafael Benítez enters the dressing room three or four minutes later; he always
gives us time to gather our thoughts on our own. He's calm, as always. He indicates
on the board that he wants to switch to 3-5-2, in part to get Steven Gerrard higher
up the pitch. Djimi Traoré is to be taken off, so he hits the showers. But then it turns
out that Steve Finnan has an injury. Finn doesn't want to be taken out. In despair he
begs Benítez to let him stay on the pitch but it's no use. The physiotherapist says
he's strained his groin and that he needs to be subbed. Traoré is called back, and he
has to dry himself off and get dressed. Dietmar Hamann is going on.

Benítez looks around. 'Is this how we want to be remembered?' He tells us that it's
a matter of pride now, what else is he going to say? We have to play for our self-
respect and for the fans who have saved up enough money to buy the expensive
tickets to watch us play tonight. I hear the singing again; it's not letting up. 'Let's just

try to score the next goal,' Benítez says. 'Then we'll see what happens.' We're listening, but we're also aware that this edition of Milan is the best in the world at defending a lead. The idea that they're going to concede three goals in one half is impossible to imagine.

Stevie is sitting next to me. As team captain, he tries to rally the troops, and he gets us screaming and shouting, but I'm certain that he and all the others are thinking the same thing as I am when we get up and head towards the grass and the stadium full of spectators: Don't let it get any worse. Spare us that. Don't let us be the team that loses 6–0 in a Champions League final. Our friends and family are watching.

2

I WASN'T LIKED AS A CHILD. THAT'S THE WAY I REMEMBER IT. I WASN'T invited to birthday parties by the other kids in the class, even though I invited them. They turned eight, nine, ten years old. I saw the invitations being handed out, practically in secret, but children pick up on things like that, particularly children faced with unpopularity day in, day out, children who find their spot in the classroom and sit there quietly. Of course I saw them, the ones who were having a party, sneaking between the rows of desks with stacks of invitations, and every time I hoped one of the envelopes was for me.

I don't know what it was about me they didn't like. I didn't bother anyone. I was a quiet boy.

We moved to Hessa, a quiet suburban island in the municipality of Ålesund, on the North Sea coast of Norway, when I was starting Year Two of school. We lived in Slinningsodden, on the very tip of Hessa. I had completed Year One in Holmestrand in Eastern Norway. I don't remember much of it, but I think it was fine. Saying that, my parents got divorced before I started school. My dad moved out. Back then my name was John Arne Eikrem. I remember sharing a room with my little brother. I was six and he was three. We had separate beds. He seemed so little, and I wanted to protect him. I also wanted to protect my dad. I felt sorry for my dad, who couldn't live with us anymore and had to move into an empty house. I thought pappa must be lonely. He only lived a couple of houses down from us, but he was alone. Some nights I couldn't stop crying. I don't know whether it was the thought of him sitting alone in the living room of his house, the fact that I missed him, or because I sometimes heard crying from my little brother's bed and I couldn't bear it. I remember Pappa coming to see us. I don't know how many times, maybe only once or twice, but I remember it clearly. Him sitting on the edge of the bed, hugging me, saying that everything was going to be all right. His smell. Him comforting my brother.

But then we moved away from him, to Hessa. That's just the way it was. I started Year Two after the summer. I was the new boy with ginger hair and freckles. Skin as white as a sheet.

Maybe that's why they didn't like me.

We didn't have much money. My mum worked two or three jobs in order to support us. We often spent the holidays at home or went on camping trips. On Hessa we lived in a red, two-storey terraced house. My little brother and I shared a room in the basement. At night you could see the lights of Ålesund city centre on the other side of the bay. But I don't remember much from my childhood. I've wiped out almost all of my childhood memories.

Mum grew up in Sunndalsøra, and she met Pappa when she started on the athletics programme in Tingvoll. These areas are all local to Ålesund. If athletic talent is inherited, mine definitely comes from her. She was a goalkeeper in the district football team, an elite gymnast and was active in track and field. She was seventeen and he was twenty when they got together. Three years later I was born, and since there was no hospital in Sunndalsøra, Mamma was driven to Molde. I came into the world on 24 September 1980. It was a long and difficult delivery. I should actually have been named Johan Arne, after my grandfather, but I'm happy it ended up being John Arne. Mum calls me Jonnen, she always has. Otherwise I'm just Riise. That's what my friends call me. Riise. I like it. I've even tattooed the name across my back. After wearing all those football jerseys with Riise on the back, I felt like it was a part of me. Part of my body.

Obviously I've read the things my mum has said about Pappa, that he hit her when he was drinking. I've read that how with me and my little brother in tow, she tried to escape him, but didn't succeed, and in the end he landed in prison. Horrible things, but I don't remember any of that happening. I don't know what did or didn't happen, but I know that he was not kind to her. Still, I have no memories of him being violent. He drank, but never in front of us kids.

There is so much from my childhood that I don't remember, so much I don't know. I haven't wanted to ask mum for fear of opening up old wounds. Why did the family move to Holmestrand when I was little? Was it because mum's oldest brother lived there, so he could protect her if necessary? All I remember is that I always had a football at my feet, the feeling of the large ball against my shoe, the sound of leather on asphalt, and that I played for my first football club in Holmestrand, and that even at the age of five or six I was better and stronger than the kids I played with. Even then I loved to shoot. I slept with the ball at night. Every morning I tried to juggle the ball all the way to school without letting it hit the ground. And on my way home.

I don't know if I erased the painful memories or if I've never had them. And because there's no way of knowing, because there's a void, then it could have been something that latched on to me when I came to the new school, I think. Children are at their most ruthless when they get wind of insecurity. Maybe they noticed something about me that I wasn't aware of, or that I thought I could hide as long as I kept quiet. I remember that I cried a lot.

The only record I have of Pappa and Mum is a photo of us sitting on a patio at a holiday camp, the three of us. I must have been six or seven. That's it.

I have one full sibling, Bjørn Helge, my brother. We've always been very close, but he doesn't want to talk about Pappa and I respect that. Then I have two half-sisters. They are Mum and Thormod's children. I was seven or so when Mum married Thormod, and I hated him when he turned up. Here he was, thinking he could take Pappa's place. But Thormod was the nicest man in the world. It can't have been easy coming into our family, with all our baggage, but he took care of us. Bjørn and I took his name: Riise. It's his name I have tattooed on my back. I have wondered about adding Eikrem too, but I haven't wanted to hurt Mum or Thormod. Mum wanted me to have Semundseth on my jersey, her family name, but I decided on Riise at an early stage. I think Mum would have been devastated if Thormod had left her, and I wanted to honour him. But Eikrem is *also* my dad's name. I have two dads. Hans Eikrem was also Pappa. And I'm older now, freer, stronger. That's why I'm considering getting a tattoo of his name, too. It might be the time for it. This is my life, my body. I decide.

3

I OFTEN FELT LONELY, SITTING ON MY OWN WITH NO ONE TO TALK TO. I had no friends to ring. When I was twelve, I started to get up at quarter to six every morning. It didn't matter if the rain was pouring, if the trees were bent over in the wind, if there was snow drifting, if the sun was shining or if it was freezing cold; I was going outside. Everyone in the house was asleep, and I changed into my tracksuit without waking anyone. Then I ran. The same route every morning, up Hessaskaret and onwards. I'd run for an hour. I often crossed paths with the newspaper carrier. I'm going to show them, I told myself. I'm going to show them. I ran for all I was worth. I thought about the kids who were mean to me at school. I have long since wiped their names from my mind, I didn't want them there, but I would picture them while I strained my body, see their faces, hear them and take on even more. My lungs could hardly cope, but I forced myself to run faster. They were bloody well going to see.

Back home I showered, and before I headed off to school I grabbed my packed lunch with the dozen or so sandwiches Mum had left for me. After school I went straight to football training with Skarbøvik/Hessa. Later I would stand outside shooting at a wooden goal that we had built in a spot right near the house, full of rocks and gravel. I had a hard shot. For hours on end I would stand there and practiSe my shot, grinding away at my technique, striking the ball at just the right spot. I worked on my strength and learned to throw the ball far. In the evening I went running again. I liked to run. It felt like payback when I raced along. It was my refuge. I was alone, which I was used to, but here I had to be alone. I loved to run. Twenty-one sessions a week. I was twelve, and if Skarbøvik/Hessa won 21-0, I might have scored nineteen of those goals. I would get the ball from the keeper, dribble past everyone and score. It was easy enough. In the end Mum rang

Aalesunds FK, the biggest club in the city, and told them that I had to train with them, but not with the kids my age. I was far too good for that, as she put it.

We've always talked like that, she and I. It's like we're in motion at all times, always moving forward. There were obstacles that had to be overcome, it was like that from the very start. There was a sense of resistance that meant we probably seemed overly cocky. Or rather, we *were* cocky. We just didn't risk gift-wrapping it, like others could take the liberty to. Our life was not like that. Our experience required us to fight for what we deserved. For that reason we probably seemed overwhelming and persistent, and we were. The people at Aalesund must have thought Mum was a fool for saying what she did, that she was just shamelessly boasting of her son's talent, as though all parents didn't do that when they contacted the club, but I *was* that good. And then the other parents got cross at the idea that I was somehow better than their child because I played in the age group up. I started to think about these parents too while I ran at the crack of dawn, the people who wanted to deny me the right to play with players who were older than me, who were a match for me. I also thought of the coaches who perhaps did not want to let me in. The menfolk were also going to see, that's what Mum called them: *the menfolk*. They were all going to see. It was Mum and I against the world.

There was a hill near where we lived, it was two or three hundred metres high. Mum stood at the top with a stopwatch. Then I sprinted up. I was given my time, then I strolled back down and sprinted up from the bottom of the hill once again. It was a monster of a hill. She screamed and hollered and urged me to push myself even harder. Over and over again I did it. Morning after morning I ran, lap after lap. I had no sporting role model. I didn't support any particular club in England or anything. This was my struggle.

4

I STOOD IN THE STREET OUTSIDE OUR RED HOUSE PLAYING KEEPY-UP, like I often did. I looked at the world around me while I stood there on the asphalt. It was February and grey. Quiet. But on this day a removals van showed up on the street. The car drove past and stopped in front of the neighbouring house. A dark-haired boy my age stepped out of the car with his parents. He just stood there looking at me. The parents started to carry furniture inside, but he came over and watched me juggling the ball. He didn't say anything, and I realised that he didn't speak Norwegian. But all that was needed was a look and a brief nod, and soon we were playing together. His name was Nikola. He and his parents had fled the war in Bosnia and ended up in the house next to ours on Slinningsodden. I was thirteen then. Soon I was eating at the Andelics' more often than at home. We felt equally excluded, the two of us. That was probably what tied us together. And football, obviously. We played all the time. In addition, things were different at their house. The food his mum and dad made didn't taste like what I got at my home. They were cooking all the time, it seemed. A lot of meat and bread. Everyone was allowed to eat with their hands. And the atmosphere during the meals was like nothing I had ever experienced. Their conversations were so loud that I often thought that they were fighting. Cigarettes everywhere. But most importantly, they were different. There was a freedom to discover, there were different ways to live, and there was a world outside Slinningsodden and Ålesund.

When I divorced for the first time, I rang Nikola and asked him to come and live with me in Liverpool. He flew straight over, planning to stay for three weeks, but he ended up staying with me for nearly two years. It was fantastic. We bought a new pool table, knocked out walls and made a big conservatory, furnished as a pool and TV-room with all kinds of games. He helped me with everything, sorted things out for me, came to the home matches at Anfield. He met his wife at the training ground right near where we lived. Amanda was a physiotherapist at Liverpool.

I think I was thirteen when I spent the summer with Pappa. It is one of the best memories I have. We hadn't seen each other for a long time. I was meant to stay for two weeks, but it ended up being four. I woke up in the morning with him in the kitchen in the house in Holmestrand, sitting and listening to the radio, holding a cigarette in one hand and a coffee cup in the other. Bread and sandwich fillings were left out for me. It was just the two of us that summer. My little brother didn't want to stay with him. Mum had sent me with a training programme that I was meant to follow all summer, but I couldn't be bothered. Pappa and I played a little football in the garden. We went swimming at the beach. We filled out football coupons together at the local shop – he was really interested in football. We often went down to a pub down by the water. My dad liked to play darts. We played against each other at the Gjesten Pub, and then we ordered *pyttipanne* – a Scandinavian dish similar to hash – and ate together. I practised day and night on a dart board in the guest room in his house in an effort to beat him, but never did. Four weeks, just the two of us. The summer of 1994. The way I remember it, the sun was shining the entire time. Of course I didn't know it back then, but after that summer we would never speak to each other again.

What I'm going to say now is probably hard to believe, but I promise it's the truth. At the end of that summer is when I decided. Not some childish whim, I really decided. It was autumn, I was only thirteen and I made a decision: I was going to be Norway's best football player of all time.

I remember getting injured in a match against boys who were two or three years older than me. I was kicked to the ground. It hurt like hell. I was driven to the emergency room, and the doctor said that there was a fracture on the outside of my foot. He said they could operate but that would mean I wouldn't be able to play football for a while. Or I could let it heal on its own. I chose the latter. I was thirteen and couldn't afford any time out at that age, I thought. That's been my thinking throughout my journey. I have to keep moving forward. I have to be the best. It might as well hurt.

5

I FITTED IN A LITTLE BETTER AT MIDDLE SCHOOL THAN I DID AT primary school. At Skarbøvika there were a couple of us who hung out, most likely because we were frozen out by the others. But I still couldn't wait to get out of there. In Year 9, I started to train with the Aalesund first team. The big star at the time was Erling Ytterland. He came from Ålesund but had played in the top division for several clubs including Vålerenga, before returning to his hometown club. I was fifteen. We trained at Nørvebana, which was a gravel pitch back then. During my first training session with the team I got the ball at my feet and Ytterland came to close me down, so I nutmegged him, then I hammered the ball in the corner of the net. I remember the players laughing and someone shouting: 'Right, welcome to the men's team, then!'

I decided to join the elite athletes programme at Fagerlia upper secondary school, even though it was a four-year programme, not the usual three years. I kind of looked forward to starting. It was a new chance – the students came from different parts of Ålesund, so they didn't know that I was the unpopular boy who nobody wanted to hang out with. I thought I could start over at the school, come in as a first-team player, the only one at the school playing on the national youth team. But at the same time I dreaded it, because I was still the same. Just as ginger, just as pale, and I still skulked around the way I always had, practically hiding under my hoody.

I played my first match for Norway's Under -15s that summer while I waited for my new life to start. On 5 July 1996 we met Sweden in Sandefjord. We lost both that and the return fixture, but later that summer we crushed Finland, and against the Finns I scored two goals. The next day I also scored against the Faroe Islands, but then so did a lot of people.

My first-team debut at Aalesunds Fotballklubb was in May the following year, and I was thrilled to get the opportunity. I was brought on as a substitute against Odd. I wore number 23, and the goal was to get a squad number from 11 and below, because back then it wasn't trendy to have a high number. In my third match, this time at home at Kråmyra Stadion, I scored three minutes after I was brought on as a substitute. But I should mention that it was against Drøbak-Frogn, and we were still floundering at the bottom of the Norwegian second division. We were playing against clubs like Eik-Tønsberg, Byåsen and Ullern. Small clubs.

At school, things started to look up. Nikola was in my class, which helped. Along with another guy from the neighbourhood, we'd become a kind of three-leaf clover. The last guy – Dan Tore Tapus – was a goalkeeper, but he went to the Latin School. Slowly I started to make some friends. Cecilie, Lise, Helene, Elisabeth, all of whom played handball, Thomas and Marius, the son of Bobbo, our manager at Aalesund. But even though I made friends, I did nothing but train. I was really dull. I don't know what the others did, but I just trained, trained and trained some more. I had to. Wearing myself out sheltered me from the outside world in some way. But just knowing that I had people who wanted to be friends with me meant a lot. Sometimes we went bowling at Moa, the shopping centre in Ålesund. But I never touched alcohol or anything else. I was already playing on the first team, so I was away a lot on the weekends. I didn't go out chasing girls. It would be a couple of years before I even kissed one.

I played nine first-team matches during the 1997 season, usually as a substitute. The next season I was a regular starter, and temporarily I was given the number 10, an important number. But we were still struggling at the bottom of the table. In August, the Nordic championship for the boys and junior teams was held in Norway. I was seventeen and had completed my second year at Fagerlia. My marks weren't bad. I had improved in maths and got a six in the oral exam and a five in the written. I've always been good at maths. I was playing in the first team, it was the middle of the season and I didn't get much of a summer holiday to speak of. The World Cup in France had finished a month earlier, and I had watched Norway beat Brazil and got lost in a daydream, hoping that one day it would be me playing in the World Cup. Ole Gunnar Solskjær, who had gone to Manchester United in the summer of 1996, had started one match and come on as a substitute in two others.

He was 25, I was seventeen. It was summer, and the radio was still playing Ricky Martin's 'La Copa de la Vida' ad infinitum.

As usual I shared a room with Magne Hoseth. He was the big star in these age-determined national youth teams. He was the undisputed number 10 and our captain, but we had just played Sweden on a pitch in Toten, with a view of Lake Mjøsa, and I had had a massive match. It was 11 August 1998. We were staying at a hotel in Hamar. We had just gone to bed when the phone rang. Magne picked up but quickly handed the receiver to me: 'It's for you.'

'For me? ... Hello?'

The man, who was speaking Swedish, said he was an agent named Anders Wallsten.

'Yeah, yeah, whatever,' I replied and hung up.

He called back, and I was convinced it was just someone messing with me. Anyway, agents weren't allowed to ring players in their rooms. 'If it's urgent, you'd better ring my mum,' I finally said.

We were almost asleep when the phone rang for a third time. This time it was Mum. She told me off, said that I should speak properly when people rang me. Then she said that the Swedish agent, who was based in Switzerland, was a scout for AS Monaco and the club wanted me to come straight down after the second leg against Sweden two days later. I remember travelling to Dokka, where the next match was to be played, and thinking: What is going on here? I mean, France had just won the World Cup, several of the players on their team that had crushed Brazil in the final in front of 80,000 mad fans at the Stade de France played for Monaco. I mean ... I was really not that good in that match against the Swedish juniors at Dokka Stadion.

A few days later we flew to Nice from Fornebu Airport. There was my mum, my uncle, an agent and me. Obviously we weren't exactly used to this. We had business-class tickets, were picked up by a driver at the airport and put up in a suite in Monte Carlo. Our luggage was taken care of. The climate was also far hotter than I was used to, and palm trees lined the streets. While my mum and the agent were in meetings – people from Aalesunds Fotballklubb were also there – I was driven to the training facility, La Turbie, which is located on a hill a little north of Monaco. And there they were, doing shooting practice: Thierry Henry and David Trezeguet. In goal was Fabien Barthez, who was dating the supermodel Linda Evangelista at the time.

I was led over to them, and they said hello to me. In addition to the boys' national team, I had played 26 first-team matches for Aalesund, that was it. My salary was 1250 kroner a month, just under £200 now, plus a free monthly travel card, and I stood there in the baking sun, 450 metres above the Riviera, shaking hands with World Cup heroes Henry, Trezeguet and Barthez.

The sporting director at Aalesund emerged from the meeting with the biggest grin I've ever seen. I realised at once that it had gone well. Aalesund were going to get 7.5million kroner upon signing, and another 7.5million when I had played fifty matches for Monaco. Fifteen million kroner – just over £2million in today's market – for a seventeen-year-old with a handful of matches at the bottom of Norway's second division. I was going to receive ten percent of the transfer fee, but I was not preoccupied by my own contract. That's the truth. I was seventeen. I liked the fact that the club offered to fly my mum and three others business class to Monaco every two weeks, putting them up in a hotel for two weeks of the month, meaning I'd only spend half of the month alone. I didn't want to be left to my own devices. Even though I had only been around for seventeen years, I had been lonely enough to last a lifetime, I thought.

I was given two days to decide. We flew back home, but I had already made my mind up – I was only going back to pack. Four days had passed since Monaco's scouts had called me at the hotel room. Everything happened insanely quickly. He had called on Tuesday night. It was Saturday. On Sunday I ate a farewell dinner with Nikola and Dan Tore. The others that I had become friends with also came to Peppes Pizza on Parkgata in the city centre. We sat by ourselves in a corner of the restaurant. They were going to start the new school year together the next morning. They were going to see each other there, without me. I was leaving to live alone in a city with strange streets. I didn't speak a word of French. I remember one of them getting up. They had made a picture for me. It was a photo of each of them glued onto a poster. Above it they had written: You have to remember us.

I'd never experienced anything like that before. That kind of friendship, love expressed in that way. I came home around ten that Sunday night. I bawled my eyes out, stormed into the living room and screamed: 'I'm not going! I'm not going!'

Mum still claims that she was the one who decided I should go. I knew that Rosenborg had been in touch and wanted me to go there, that I could move to

Trondheim and start school there. I tried to reason that it was a better alternative, then I wouldn't have to move so far away. Then I could come to Ålesund on the weekends.

Mum was firm, but she was not the one who made the call. I went through the advantages and disadvantages with my brother in the bedroom. We rattled them off. Before I went to sleep, I said to him: 'So it's a no, then.' 'Yes,' he said, 'it's a no.'

That night I had a dream, a dream of me running into a stadium. It was packed, and the fans roared when they spotted me. Everyone looked at me and I got goose pimples all over my body. The feeling was better than anything I had ever experienced.

I woke up before anyone else in the house. I went straight to my mum, it was five or six o'clock in the morning, I remember her dishevelled head poking up from under the duvet. 'We have to go.'

The plane was taking off in only a few hours.

On the way to the airport we stopped at the school. I stood by the teacher's desk and said goodbye to the class. On the plane, my face was white as a sheet. I didn't want to sit next to my mum. Grandma was with us, too. I didn't want to talk to anyone. I sat on my own and looked out the window, saw the city with all my friends disappear beneath me. Then I cried. It's still painful to think about it. I was just a child, and I was going to be alone again, like I had been for most of my life.

6

I LIVED IN A HOTEL FOR THREE MONTHS – LE MÉRIDIEN – BEFORE MOVING into a studio flat that was fourteen square metres. Not that I suffered any distress in that respect – the balcony was fifteen square metres and had a direct view of the famous Monte Carlo casino just down the street. I never went, I've still never been. I didn't go out much. I should have strolled around the harbour and checked out the luxury yachts or the cars outside the casino, the rows of Ferraris, Bentleys, Rolls Royces and everything else there, especially since I'm so fascinated by cars. But I mostly sat inside playing video games. I sat there, in a practically empty studio flat, with a big screen. Only one of my teammates spoke English when I arrived: a guy from Portugal named Costinha, a defensive midfielder who was six years older than me. He was a big help.

I started to train with the first team right away. I was not sent to the development squad or the youth team first, as I had expected. At the very first training session the team had to complete a running test. That was something I could do, it was just a matter of running. All the mornings running around Slinningsodden, I figured, had helped.

The sun was at its peak. It was over forty degrees. Normally I would have taken a position at the front, instead I found a place in the middle of the pack, thinking I should hang back a little. I didn't even know how far we were supposed to run. I didn't know the drill and didn't understand what was being said. The stars didn't last very long, this wasn't something they needed to be good at, but soon more players started to slow up. I continued to hold back, seeing the squad thin out in front of me. People dropped off one by one. We ran round and round. I could see Henry and Trezeguet and the others sat down drinking water and watching us. I sensed they were following me extra close, the new guy who was only seventeen years old. Now there were two, three, four of us in a row and I realised what the drill was all about. We had to run until we couldn't run anymore. So I picked up the pace. In the end there was only one other person who could stay with me, one of the Senegalese players in the squad, Moussa N'Diaye. But I was really going now, I had loads of energy, and the others were observing from the sidelines. In the end the manager had to intervene: 'Stop, stop!' he shouted.

Afterwards we did a few quick ball drills. I noticed the others grabbing a drink from the water bottles, but I didn't dare. I didn't know if the manager allowed it. I didn't want to do anything that wasn't allowed during my first training session as a professional football player, so I didn't have a drop of water.

But my running had gained me the respect of the others. The stars came over and we exchanged a few words. They nodded in acknowledgement and from their looks I could see that they were impressed. In the dressing room I felt that I was accepted almost immediately.

In one of my first training sessions we had shooting practice. I had a hard shot, I really did. On this occasion I struck one ball particularly cleanly, and Fabien Barthez threw himself to the ground to stop it. He got a hand on the ball and shouted in pain. He had a small fracture in his wrist, and had to tape it up for the first part of the season.

The manager, the former French international, Jean Tigana, was happy with my efforts, but he didn't speak English. I remember when I was going to make my first start. It was against Bastia in Corsica in November 1998. 'You play left.' That was all he said. Where on the left? On the left of defence, in midfield, in attack? It turned out that he'd meant for me to play left of the two central midfielders. That became clear from all his gesticulating once the match had started. I got a yellow card. We lost 3–1, but I soon learned French. I've always had a good ear for languages. The next match I started was against Nancy, two league matches later. We won 3–0.

I'm not fond of being alone. It makes me feel insecure. Despite the regular visits from Norway I often felt lonely. I'd sit on my bed wondering why Pappa hadn't contacted me, especially now I had become a pro. He was so obsessed by football, so he must have been proud. More than four years had passed since our summer together in Holmestrand. Not a peep from him. But I told myself that maybe it was normal because of the divorce and everything that had happened between him and Mum.

Also, this was before text messages, it was not simply a matter of sending off a quick message or a congratulations, it required more to contact someone.

A lot of know-it-alls had cried foul, stating that I was far too young to travel abroad. For example, the head of talent at the Football Association of Norway told the newspapers that he didn't think I was ready for Monaco, that the move could put a brutal end to my career. A lot of people said things like that. And something inside me obviously thought that they might be right, not least when I was sitting alone in the studio flat on the third floor. After all they were older and had experienced more than I had. I was just a seventeen-year-old boy when I left. But another part of me thought: Damn it, I'll show you. I'll make them shut their traps. What they said annoyed me to no end, and that thought helped me to hold out. I soon realised: I'm strong. I can adjust. I can live according to where I am. They're not going to come and tell me that they know what I can and can't handle. I decide that.

I obtained my driving licence in Monte Carlo when I turned eighteen. It's quite possible that the club exercised a certain influence over the driving test, because I managed on two hours of theory and one hour of driver training. To be fair I had played a lot of car games. As for the theory test, it might have helped that I sneaked a peek at the guy next to me and answered the same as him when I was uncertain. Straight away I bought a BMW Z3M. A convertible, of course; big and impractical in the narrow streets of Monte Carlo. The following year I bought a Mercedes convertible, also far too big and impractical. I was earning 300,000 kroner (just over £45,000 today) a month tax-free, not a huge amount, but I didn't have much else to spend it on. As a four-seater, the Mercedes was considered a family car.

One day in February 1999 one of the club's directors hurried out onto the training pitch. I had been at the club for five months, but had never spoken to him previously, so I was surprised when he asked to talk to me. 'It's your father,' he said.

'My dad?' I said.

'I think you have to go home now.'

I don't know why, but I instinctively realised that it was my biological father he was talking about. I don't think I knew that he was ill until that day, when I was told that he had been diagnosed with lymphoma, a form of cancer that begins in infection-fighting cells of the immune system. It was no longer treatable. He was hospitalised with double pneumonia, and his body couldn't take much more. I showered and changed into my official Monaco training gear. I wanted him to have a chance to see me wearing it. I was driven to the airport in Nice, and the ride there, check-in, security, and the three-hour flight are all fuzzy in my mind. I was picked up by my mum when I landed in Oslo. Pappa was in the hospital in Tønsberg, 100km south. We stopped at my uncle's place in Holmestrand to grab something to eat on the way. It was dark outside, late evening. Cold.

Inside the hospital, in the sharply lit corridors, a nurse greeted us: 'I'm glad you made it. He really wants to see you,' she said to me, then she went into the room ahead of me. I heard her say inside: 'He's here now.' I hadn't seen or spoken to my dad for four and a half years. Now he was on his deathbed. We were finally going to see each other again after such a long time, and at the same time we had to say goodbye.

I walked through the door, into the room where he lay. At that very moment – when I set foot inside – I could hear the heart machine flatten out. Beeeeep. I didn't even make it over to him. He was dead. I remember someone saying it.

'Is he dead?' I heard myself asking.

'Yes, I'm sorry.'

I had stopped on the way for a bite to eat.

I was completely beside myself with rage and sorrow. I grabbed things around me — an office chair, a bed, a trolley – pushed them away, knocked them over, shoved them away and screamed, while the nurse tried to hold me, stop me. I cried like I had never cried before.

I don't know how long afterwards it was, but I went in to see my dad. He was just lying there. I barely recognised him. His hands were on top of the duvet, all bones, and his face was ravaged by illness. He had sunken cheeks and hollow eyes.

I stood there in front of his lifeless body, in my official red and white training kit with the club emblem on the chest. I think we could have become good friends. If he had had a chance to accompany me further with what was about to happen with me and my career, we would have grown close. It could have been good between us. That's what I believe. Not now. That opportunity no longer existed, and it never would. It is a great loss. The sense of loss only gets stronger. Still, I can hardly believe that he died when I walked through the door. It was Friday, 19 February 1999. He was forty years old.

I didn't want to grieve. The following morning I went straight from the hospital back to Monaco. I started to train again straight away, and it felt like the comfort it always had been. I didn't speak to anyone, I still couldn't speak the language well enough. I sat in my flat. I didn't cry. On Thursday I started the away match against Montpellier.

That season we ended up fourth in the league.

I wish I had memories from Pappa's funeral. I would have liked to know what was said about him, to have had memories of the coffin and to have seen the flowers. He was my dad. I have to remember the good things. I don't know why he didn't reach out to me. As a boy I wondered from time to time if that meant he didn't love me. He never said: I love you. He wasn't like that.

I didn't go to his funeral. I regret that. I don't even know where he is buried. Truth be told, I don't know the most basic things about my dad. I don't know where he came from, where he grew up, I'm not even certain what he did for a living. I've never spoke to or saw my grandfather or grandmother after the divorce, and I don't actually want to call them grandfather and grandmother, they were Pappa's parents. I don't even know if they're alive. I was a small child when I last saw them. It's strange, but despite all of this I feel somewhere that I am an Eikrem. I refuse to be embarrassed by it. My name is Riise, and I love Thormod, he knows that, but I'm also my dad's son.

Mum was the one who decided that we weren't going to the funeral. I am angry at her for that, even though I understand her. There was a lot of bad blood between the families. After Pappa's funeral his parents demanded that I pay for it, for the coffin, the food, everything. They thought as a professional football player, I could afford it. Mum didn't want me to, and that wasn't right either. I was an eighteen-year-old who had just lost his dad. I don't know at which church the funeral was held. I have started to search for the grave. When I find it, I'm going to go there and leave a flower.

One Christmas after my dad died, my mum sent me a photo album with pictures from my childhood. It's one of the few things I've taken with me when I've changed clubs and moved to a new country. In the album there is a picture of my dad lying on the floor and hugging me. I'm just a baby. It's scary to see how much he resembles me. As adults we're completely alike. It's the one photo I always keep on my mobile.

7

IT WAS WEDNESDAY 16 FEBRUARY 2000, MY FIRST GOAL FOR MONACO, and it came from 35 yards. I was into my second season at the club – 1999/2000 – and we were very good. We were helped by the signing of Mexican defender Rafael Márquez, who would later become a key figure at Barcelona. I was rewarded for the efforts of my debut season with a hike in wages, and I was given jersey number 3 instead of 28. Even after Tigana left the club in January 1999, I was given a lot of trust by his replacement, Claude Puel, someone who would later manage Southampton and Leicester City. I was one of the form players when winter arrived. Not long before my goal against Bordeaux I fired off a volley from 35 yards against Rennes that struck the crossbar. After the match, Barthez said that I could just have strolled off the pitch if the ball had gone in.

At the same time I was selected for the senior men's national team for the first time and played my first match against Iceland in La Manga. It was 0–0, but the newspapers wrote that I was a find for Nils Johan Semb, and could go directly into the European Championship team for the summer.

On 15 February, I was selected for the national team again, and I was over the moon. Whereas La Manga had been a squad without many of its biggest names, all the presumed best players had been called up this time. We were to meet Turkey in Istanbul as the first proper warm-up match for the European Championship. I didn't know what I dared to hope for. On the one hand I was among the best physically, maybe the best. I had a left foot like nobody else. I was mentally strong, had a fierce willpower, was energetic and hyper. But I also felt like a child. I felt small. I knew that I had to seize the opportunity. When you're young, a long time can pass before you get another chance to prove yourself if you don't pass the test. The match against

Turkey was my opportunity to show myself. There was one thing I dreamed of more than anything else: to play in a tournament for Norway.

The day after my selection I got to celebrate properly. I got a fresh chance at Monaco. In the match against Bordeaux, one of the other teams at the top, I was brought on with all of a quarter of an hour remaining. The league was drawing towards an end, it was getting close. It was 0–0. We were playing at home. Our team had been pressing the entire match, but Bordeaux stood firm, including a save off the line after an attempt by David Trezeguet. With seven minutes remaining, sure enough a long clearance came from Bordeaux's defence, the ball was nodded towards the centre of the pitch by Costinha, and I saw it come shooting from the right towards me. I don't know exactly what I was thinking. I had just taken a few steps out of the centre circle. But then I hammered it with my left foot. And the ball flew in from 35 yards. In the dressing room afterwards Barthez went down on all fours and kissed my left foot. All the papers wrote about the goal the next day: *Le Monde, Le Figaro*. A photo of my celebration was spread over the entire front page of the sports paper *L'Équipe*. The customs officers and flight attendants wanted to talk to me about the goal when I flew to Norway. The chief executive at Monaco said that I was going to be a superstar in France after this. It was a key away victory on our road to winning the league, seven points ahead of second-place Paris Saint-Germain. Prince Albert put ten to fifteen Porsche convertibles at our disposal, which the players could drive around in to celebrate. I was nineteen years old. It was a goal that was shown all over the world, it was that kind of goal. *Hello, world! Here I am! Boom! That's for those of you who doubted me!*

After that I started to walk a little taller when I strolled around the city. I became a slightly different person. I had met a girlfriend who I would end up marrying. Big clubs around the world had my name in their notepad. Arsène Wenger at Arsenal and Sir Alex Ferguson at Manchester United were also meant to be interested. According to rumours, David O'Leary at Leeds United wanted to buy me. Enormous sums were mentioned. But that was not what consumed me. The national team were going to meet Turkey. I gave my all in the training sessions, then I collected balls and carried kit. I was still the newcomer. But I got the chance to start on the left flank. I remember I kept throwing up before I went on the pitch at the Ali Sami Yen stadium in Istanbul. I was in top shape, but I was so nervous.

It felt like now or never. A European Championship tournament awaited me in the summer. I had to distinguish myself. After 38 minutes I scored the first goal of the match, my first goal for the national team.

8

I WAS ONLY NINETEEN WHEN I FOUND OUT I WAS GOING TO BE A DAD. It was May 2000. I thought it was fantastic news. Guri and I had met during the summer of 1999. I'd been back home on holiday, and she was the kind of girl that all the guys and girls knew. Ålesund is not a big city, but she was also very attractive. She worked as an aerobics instructor, and I managed to persuade Nikola to sign up to one of her classes with me. And yes, we were definitely the only guys in the room. Previously I wouldn't have had a chance with a girl like her, but now was I a different person, and I acted differently. I was more confident. And there was no doubt that people looked at me in a new way now that I was in the papers. Guri and I started dating, and pretty soon after she moved in with me in Monaco. And then Ariana came along. I was happy. I wanted to start a family early, maybe it's because I wanted to guard myself against being alone, I don't know. Maybe because I had some sense of loss that came from the family that existed when I was very little, and which I didn't have any memories of. I wanted a family. The Semundseth family had shown me how close a family could be. Mum, the second youngest of five, spoke to her sisters and brothers every single day; she probably still does. I wanted to have my people around me, and I didn't care if a part of my family thought it was stupid, that I was too young. I was going to be a dad. I was happy and I was terrified, but I knew that I was kind and considerate, and when Ariana arrived on 2 January 2001, she was the most beautiful thing I had ever seen.

At the European Championships with Norway, just four months after the cannon of a shot against Bordeaux, things didn't go too well for me. I was selected for the squad and played in all the warm-up matches, albeit as a substitute for John Carew in the final two, but when the real fun got started in the Netherlands and Belgium in June, I didn't get to play one minute. I was so bloody disappointed. And I have to say, to this day I think the manager, Nils Johan Semb, was cautious in his decision not to pick me. I like Semb, and I have a lot to thank him for, but I had played well in the build-up. It was only my age that spoke against me. Sure, I had a lot to learn, but I was good enough. I wasn't there as an apprentice, I was there to play. Stig Inge Bjørnebye, who was the last to be selected for the squad, hadn't even been part of the meetings in advance, but was still preferred to me when Vegard Heggem pulled a muscle against Yugoslavia. I was nineteen, and I had to respect the decision. I continued to collect balls and carry kit. I did it for some time too. I said nothing. Ole Gunnar Solskjær, maybe the biggest star on the team – only the previous year he had won a Champions League final for Manchester United – played all the matches from the start, without scoring. My plan was to be Norway's best footballer ever, and Solskjær might be the only player who still sits above me in that regard, but I was in no way obsessed by these things on the national team in 2000. I admired him. He was one of the older teammates that I looked up to. I tried to show my best side in training sessions. I wanted to convince him and the others with more experience that I was good enough. I remember that just for fun I nutmegged Solskjær when we were playing five on five. He just kicked me. He was furious. I was scared that I had gone too far and acted disrespectfully. I hoped I hadn't ruined things for myself. I knew my place. All I wanted was for them to like me.

I sat in an outdoor space in Oslo with a big screen and watched the final and saw my teammate David Trezeguet thump in the decisive goal in extra time, meaning France beat Italy on the golden goal rule. After that he was sold to Juventus. Maybe all of this was an omen. In the 2000/01 season Monaco did far worse. I didn't get to play much either, just sixteen times in the league, something which to a large extent was probably due to my own big mouth. Prior to the season I was open about wanting to go to England. I was inexperienced, and the desire to get away did not go down well. Both Fulham and Leeds made an offer to Monaco to buy me for £4million but the club scared off the suitors by demanding an additional £2million. My relationship with the club did not exactly improve. I was frozen out. The coach said he prioritised experience. We finished in eleventh place in the league.

9

I SAT IN JEAN TIGANA'S VINEYARD EAST OF MARSEILLE. EVERYTHING was ready. Tigana had taken over at Fulham after being offered a monster contract by the Egyptian owner of Harrods, Mohamed Al-Fayed, and during his first season had led the team to promotion to the Premier League. Now they needed to strengthen the squad ahead of playing in the top flight. It was June 2001. He wanted to bring me to the club. The sporting director of the London club was also there, as well as Mum and my new agent, Einar Baardsen. For me, all that remained was to read through the contract, and I pretended to do just that, but actually I had just planned on signing anyway. I held the pen, was about to place the tip of the pen on the paper, when a mobile rang. It was my agent's mobile. He left the room to take the call, and I was left waiting for him to return. It was a magnificent and impressive holiday home. The sun shone through the windows. When Baardsen returned, I stood up and he whispered in my ear: 'That was Liverpool. They were wondering if you had signed for Fulham. If not, they want you to fly there immediately.'

I looked at him, before looking at the others in the room who were watching us. 'All right.'

'Yes.'

I hate disappointing people. There was such a nice atmosphere in the room. Everyone smiling and laughing, chatting. This was the manager who had given me my first chance as a professional footballer in a foreign climate. I looked at the exit. Then I told my agent, while nodding in the direction of the others: 'Ok, you take care of this,' before I walked out to the car. The others must have wondered what was going on, but I just climbed into the back seat and waited. I was embarrassed. But hey, this was Liverpool. I had to do it, even though it meant acting like a fool. I didn't even say a proper goodbye.

10

AT LIVERPOOL AIRPORT, BEFORE IT WAS RENAMED JOHN LENNON Airport, we were picked up by a driver. The June sun stood high in the sky on that Monday in 2001. Phil Thompson, a defensive giant from the great teams of the 1970s and 1980s, was now assistant manager, and he met us at the stadium, Anfield. Gérard Houllier had managed Liverpool since 1998. With his five-year plan he was determined to return the team to the top, among other things by instilling strict discipline. The Liverpool team had acquired a bad reputation during the 90s. The press had disparagingly dubbed the players the Spice Boys, a play on the Spice Girls, with the intimation that they were highly paid but didn't perform. More stars than football players, undoubtedly talented, but unwilling to do the dirty work needed to be the best. That was probably the notion they were trying to convey.

When we arrived in the city, I remember still having doubts about whether my agent had understood things correctly. I was rather confused. Imagine if he had been mistaken. Those doubts soon vanished when someone handed me the daily paper and there was an article about the club considering buying a young Norwegian with a brilliant left foot, that I was going to complete a medical that day, and that only minor details remained in the negotiations between Liverpool and Monaco.

When I arrived at Anfield, there was already a group of children waiting to get an autograph from the latest signing. Only at that point did I seriously begin to realise that it had to be true, and soon I was being shown around by Houllier while the contract was being negotiated. We drove to Liverpool's historic training ground, Melwood, which was rather run-down but in the process of being upgraded into a state-of-the-art facility according to Houllier's guidelines. Back at Anfield – in an effort to seal the deal – he brought me out on the pitch. The stadium was empty. It was just us, surrounded by the empty red seats. We stood in the middle of

The Kop, the stand where the core of the Liverpool supporters sat. All was quiet. It was obviously a gimmick, but irresistible all the same. He spread out his arms and simply asked me: 'Do you want to play here?'

I was twenty years old and I signed a five-year contract. It was the same summer Zlatan Ibrahimović was sold to Ajax. He was a year younger and a little more expensive, but I was a wing-back and still went for £4million. Nothing to be ashamed of.

I fitted the profile of the sort of player Houllier wanted in his team. Yes, he wanted to use me as a left midfielder to start with, even though I felt most comfortable as a left-back, but that wasn't important to me. He knew that I trained hard and selflessly. I played with passion and was loyal. I didn't drink. While my teammates at Monaco had wine with their meals, I had mineral water. I had also started a family so I mostly stayed at home with them. In Monaco I never let myself get mixed up in the rivalry over who had the biggest house, or the wife with the nicest jewellery. I played football, then went home to be with my family. I liked to run. I liked to lift weights. I liked to do the work, quite simply. It brought back good memories from running back home around Slinningsodden, the feeling of being my own man.

The week before I went to Liverpool to start the build-up to the season, I trained like a beast in Monte Carlo. I lifted weights and raced along the streets of the small city like a madman, pavement after pavement, until people smiled and laughed at me when I passed. Then I went out to run somewhere where it was less flat. I knew I was moving to the most physically demanding league in the world. There were crunching tackles in England. The tempo, the intensity and the pressure were completely different from what I had experienced in the French league. I wanted to turn up prepared and stronger than ever.

I remember really dreading the first training session with my new teammates. Who was I, really? A young lad who had not even been a regular on a team that finished eleventh in the French league. Not that they knew anything about it. Why would they care?

I didn't say much when I entered the dressing room. I don't think I looked any of them directly in the eye. I was completely exposed. There they were, the stars I recognised from the TV: Michael Owen. Jamie Carragher. Steven Gerrard. I was allocated a spot, started to get changed and tried to keep one thought at bay:

What are you doing here?

They didn't say much to me either. They were used to having players show up, have a go, only to disappear again. You have to prove yourself first. And they watch what you're doing. I knew that. All 25 members of the squad followed everything I did like a hawk. If a touch was too heavy, a pass imprecise, a tackle too hard, they'd notice. They'd keep an eye on you in the dressing room as well: was I too cocky, too evasive, awkward or insecure? As a new player, did I show enough respect to them, yet enough disrespect during a match? *Should we take him to a training session and see if he copes?* That's how it is. Twenty-five people staring at you. I was a nobody. But I could be a somebody. It was all up to me.

Luckily the first part of the training session was a running drill. For 45 minutes we had to run. In contrast to Monaco, I knew the language and knew straight away what I was supposed to do, so when the whistle blew, I scurried off. I raced away from everyone at the start. I heard Robbie Fowler behind me say, 'We'll catch him later.' They didn't. And they realised that I was someone who had to be taken seriously. At the first training camp with Liverpool – in Bad Ragaz in Switzerland – the same thing happened. We had to run as far as we could for six minutes. I beat the next person – Patrik Berger – by 25 yards. Jamie Redknapp nicknamed me the 'The Machine'. Not too flashy, I suppose, but being considered strong and tenacious was exactly what I wanted my reputation to be. To my ears it sounded perfect. Presumably Houllier felt the same. I liked his rules. We had to have our mobiles switched off during the entire pre-match activities. We could only have them switched on in our hotel rooms; not in the corridors, not in the lobby. Being a Liverpool player carried a certain responsibility, and a lot of attention. When we went on our tour of Asia, thousands of fans greeted us when we got off the plane in Singapore, even though it was not even six o'clock in the morning. Even more were waiting outside our hotel. In Bangkok we were met by 1,500 screaming fans and five busloads of riot police. There were upwards of 80,000 people – at our training session. What did I think? That's the way, Riise. That's how life is meant to be.

At night I read up on my teammates in an effort to work better with them. I tried to watch and listen. Who talks a lot? Who is quiet? On the way back from Asia, Robbie Fowler sprayed shaving foam in my hair while I slept. I didn't think it was particularly funny but I didn't complain. If anything, it was possible some of the older players thought I was too hyper. Maybe a few interpreted it as me being overly ambitious or childish, but that's how I am when I feel confident. Every morning when I get out of bed I'm wide awake. I'm ready. C'mon. Anyone?

11

GOD, WAS I NERVOUS. I THOUGHT I WAS GOING TO THROW UP. I STOOD in the players' tunnel at the Millennium Stadium in Cardiff, Wales. For the first time I was going to appear in front of the English footballing public. In Monaco, the fans sat rather quietly during matches, applauded politely, but I could hear 70,000 mad Brits from the tunnel. The roof was closed, something that made for an even more oppressive and charged atmosphere.

It was Sunday, 12 August 2001, and I was selected to play in Liverpool's first game of the season, the Charity Shield. I had been given the number 18, which a few years before had been Michael Owen's number when he joined Liverpool's first team. Owen was now Liverpool's number 10. As FA Cup holders we were facing Manchester United, who the previous season had won the league by ten points. I had performed well in pre-season, but I was young, new to the club and by no means considered a regular on the team. I was not the first choice. Houllier had taken me aside and said that he would be incredibly pleased if I played fifteen matches over the course of the season in total, including substitutions. The fact that I was picked to start this match was most likely a tactical move on his part, to build up my self-confidence.

I remember the roar when we came out on the pitch, how both teams' players lined up in the middle, and we greeted each other one by one. I was there, both sets of fans singing, and I greeted opponents such as David Beckham, Ryan Giggs, Paul Scholes and my old teammate Fabien Barthez.

Before two minutes had elapsed, Roy Keane brought down Danny Murphy in the box. Gary McAllister placed the penalty safely in the bottom left corner and we led 1–0. A little later I got a little space on the left and was able to hit a hard cross which

Nicky Butt nearly headed into his own goal. Soon Michael Owen broke free after Emile Heskey won a header against Jaap Stam, and we led 2–0 inside twenty minutes. We ended up winning 2–1, and what can I say, I had Ruud van Nistelrooy and Beckham under complete control on my flank. I was on my way.

For the time being Guri, Ariana and I were living in a block of flats owned by Liverpool, where they housed the new players so they could look after them. I became friends with Sami Hyypiä almost immediately. He took care of me, invited us to his place to meet his family, making it easier to adjust to the new city.

Three days later I left for Oslo to play an international friendly against Turkey. It was an insignificant match. John Carew missed a penalty, Tore André Flo missed an open goal, and it ended 1–1. I was voted man of the match by several newspapers, but that's not the reason I mention it.

After the game, a number of the players met in the sky bar at the top of the SAS hotel on Holbergs Plass, where we were staying. I sat with Steffen Iversen, my friend on the national team. We shared a room. He wondered why I didn't drink alcohol, and I replied that I didn't like the taste.

'Have you ever tried?'

'No.'

'Not even a taste?'

'Just a little sip, enough to know I don't like it.'

'But if you mix vodka with orange juice, then you can't even taste it,' he said and I agreed to try a single vodka and orange juice. He was right about it, I couldn't taste the alcohol. I had another one. But soon – without realising it – Steffen was ordering doubles instead of singles to surprise me, and when we continued on to the nightclub Smuget, I could hardly walk. I had to find the loo as soon as we got inside, and I was left bent over a toilet bowl throwing up. After a while, Steffen came in. He'd been looking for me. The press had apparently got wind of the fact that I was pissed, someone had called them, so Steffen got me on my feet and helped me outside, got me in a taxi and back to my room. I'll give him that, Steffen.

The next day I had to get up at five in the morning to catch a flight. As if that wasn't bad enough, I was going to have Morten Pedersen, a journalist from *Dagbladet* in tow the entire way to Liverpool. We had arranged it a long time ago.

He didn't like me, it was clear from what he wrote about me, and I had invited him in the hope that we could square things up. We had to check in together, sit next to each other on the plane. He was going to come to my flat, where I planned to make something simple for us to eat, before taking him to a training session. I'd wanted to put my best self forward.

I was in a really bad way. Even the stewardess pointed it out: 'Poor lad. So good yesterday, so bad today.' I threw up four times on the stretch to Copenhagen alone. And I chatted and tried to explain it away to Pedersen: 'The problem is that I can't sleep after matches. I don't get any peace – no rest. And when you have to get up at the crack of dawn, and catch a flight on top of that, things go wrong. Like now.' But I had a terrible hangover, and on the afternoon that day I had a training session with Liverpool.

'John!' I recognised the French accent of Gérard Houllier. The door to his office was open. He always came across as being calm, but he could get quite angry, he really could. I was brand new at the club and was overcome with anxiety. Hanging from his office wall, the club values were framed in glass: Show respect. Be a winner. Think of the team first. Always be a top professional.

I don't know how he found out what had happened. It was two days before our first league match against West Ham. I was given a long speech about what would happen if I did that again. So much for the disciplined Norwegian. Me, the guy who had never touched a drop of alcohol in his life. I thought I was going to have to wait a long time to see those fifteen matches.

But I came on in the second half against West Ham United to make my league debut in front of a sold-out Anfield. The feeling is impossible to describe. I did well for myself, but things went even better when we met Bayern Munich in the UEFA Super Cup six days later. As UEFA Cup holders we were facing the winners of the Champions League. Chance would have it that the match took place on my old home turf in Monaco, Stade Louis II. I may not have played much in my final season there, but I was back, and I was in the starting eleven. Inside 25 minutes I scored the first goal of the match past Oliver Kahn. We won 3–2, with Emile Heskey and Michael Owen also getting one each.

I was twenty years old and had scored for Liverpool in the Super Cup against Bayern Munich. I had arrived. All the hard work had paid off. All the runs up the monster hill back home. All the late training sessions. All the pain, the sacrifices, and the fear of not being good enough. The lonely nights in Monaco. I had done it. I had shown them.

A few days later I heard reports from back home in Ålesund of people watching Liverpool matches at Miller's pub. Middle-aged men sitting in their Liverpool jerseys, shouting when I came on against Bolton Wanderers a few weeks later: 'No! No, not him! Why have they put him out there? Are they going to send his mum on, too? Now we definitely won't win!'

Me, a twenty-year-old lad from their own town who got to play for the club they loved? I tried not to think about it too much. I tried to act tough. 'If that's how they feel ...' But I couldn't help wondering: What was it about me that was so difficult to like?

12

I DON'T KNOW EXACTLY HOW FAR IN ADVANCE THE LADS STARTED TO speak about the Merseyside derby, but I do know it was early. The entire city was seething two or three weeks prior to the match. Everywhere people were chatting about it, on the streets, in the cafes, in the shops and pubs. I'd been told that I was going to start. My mum was going to be at the match. Nikola was travelling from Ålesund. The papers in Liverpool wrote about nothing but the match. As a player, I could hardly move when I went outside. The pressure was insane. The two stadiums are just a couple of hundred yards from each other. The local lads on the team repeated over and over again: losing to Everton cannot happen.

It was two weeks after the match against Bolton. We hadn't opened well in the league and needed a win, even though it was away at Goodison Park. It was hot. The sun was high in the sky. Twelve o'clock kick-off. I was going to play on the left flank.

I remember the roar from the crowd. I remember the songs. I was a long way from Miller's pub. Everton took an early lead after Kevin Campbell managed to turn and get a shot off in the penalty area, but Steven Gerrard soon levelled and celebrated by running towards the home fans with his hand to his ear before sticking out his tongue and pointing to the name on the back of his strip.

Michael Owen scored the penalty we were awarded before half-time after Emile Heskey was brought down, and with that we took the lead. But the next thing to happen, I can hardly explain. Seven minutes into the second half Sami Hyypiä nods the ball out of our own penalty area. Danny Murphy hits it ahead to me on the left. I start from our own half, touch the ball for the first time on the halfway line, race ahead. I see Emile Heskey on the opposite side, but he's covered. Instead I keep driving the ball towards their right-back. He retreats. I move closer and closer. I'm almost in shooting range. I feinted one step to the inside and the right-back bites.

Then I spin to the outside again. He tries to kick the ball away, but I nutmeg him and he is completely gone. Now I start to feel that I have sprinted a good way. My thighs are burning. But I'm inside the penalty area and I get off a shot. It's not a cannon, but it's hard enough and it goes low in the far corner. My first goal in the Premier League. A solo raid. Delirious, I ran towards the corner where I knew mum and Nikola were sitting, in row ten, pulled my jersey over my head in joy and slid down on my knees. It was not a celebration that I had planned. Only natural goalscorers plan celebrations. But if there was ever a goal to pull your jersey over the head for, this was it.

The following week I heard The Kop singing over and over again:

John Arne Riise, John Arne Riise,
Ran half the pitch to score at the pit.
And we sang
And we laughed
And we shook the ground that's made of wood
John Arne Riise
Scored against the Shite.

They had made their first song about me.

We won 3–1. When I was substituted towards the end of the match, I received a standing ovation. That goal did everything for me. Several newspapers selected me as man of the match. I was interviewed by everyone. The song was made into a ring-tone that you could buy, and several times when I was out somewhere, I would suddenly hear it when someone took a call. Strange things like that.

After the match I sat in the visiting dressing room for a while. I tried to take it all in while players like Gerrard, Carragher and Owen stood around me getting ready. Everyone was happy. I felt I had to learn from this incredible thing that had happened to me, make some sense out of the magic. What could I do to make something similar happen again? I went through my pre-match preparations in detail. I recalled exactly how I had got changed. I had put on my left sock first, then the right. The left shoe before the right. During the warm-up I had not worn my shin guards. I had put them on later, then wound the tape around the socks. As always, I had tied the left shoe a little tighter than the right, and after the warm-up I had re-tied my laces, just to be sure.

I got dressed, put the deodorant and gel in my toilet bag. From now on, I thought, I am going to prepare exactly the same way before every single match. I was happy, and that was a way to increase my chances of being just as happy in the future.

I bought a house from Christian Ziege, meaning it passed from one left-back to another. After one season at Liverpool he joined Tottenham Hotspur. The house was in Woolton, a lovely middle-class suburb, in a gated community where there were seven or eight other houses. 400 square metres spread out over three floors, with five bathrooms and six bedrooms, one of which I converted into an office. I was 21 years old, a home-owner and a father. I was a Liverpool player. I had scored a solo goal on my derby debut against Everton. I signed autographs for anyone who wanted one. I was named in the team of the month in a selection carried out by Europe's seven leading sports magazines, preferred at left-back over players like Paolo Maldini and Roberto Carlos. I had a song made about me by the supporters, and it was played on mobiles when people rang each other. Sure, I drove a worn-out Vauxhall that had been supplied by the club, but at Christmas I was going to buy a BMW X5 with tinted windows, a family car. Like the rest of the team, apart from Jamie Carragher who was born in Bootle and wedded to the area, we went to the Trafford Centre, the huge shopping centre on the outskirts of Manchester, to avoid getting stopped all the time. Things could not have been better for me.

13

I HAVE A BLACK BOX WHERE I STORE ALL MY BAD MEMORIES IN MY mind. The box has a key, which I can use to unlock and hide a new memory in there, but I can't take out old ones. Once the memory is locked away, it disappears inside the darkness it deserves. That's how I see it. That's why the box is black. Everything inside is horrible and awful.

Keeping these memories in a box feels safe. Still, if I have the key to unlock the box, shouldn't I be able to take something out, too?

I've been betrayed. I've been beaten down. And I've done a lot of stupid things. I don't live with any of my children.

I'm not used to thinking about the darkness. I don't like it. Instead I pull away, like when a player is receiving treatment after a fall or remains on the ground after a violent coming together; I prefer not to look. I stay away. I try to keep the light switched on in my life.

14

THE ONLY MATCHES THAT MEASURE UP TO DERBIES AGAINST
Everton are clashes with Manchester United. Phil Chisnall is the last player to
have moved directly from one club to the other when he signed for Liverpool from
the Red Devils in 1964. It's virtually unthinkable for a Liverpool player to move to
Manchester United. The most famous example is Michael Owen, but he had played
for Real Madrid in the meantime, had suffered a devastating knee injury and arrived
on a free transfer from Newcastle United, without being able reach the levels he
set at Liverpool. Personally, I thought it was a very odd choice for a Liverpool lad.
Even I would never play for Manchester United. No chance. Just the thought is
terrifying. I'm like Steven Gerrard in that regard. Over his long career he has
collected an impressive number of opponents' jerseys at his home. But there are
none from Manchester United. He wouldn't have them in his home. That's how
strong the rivalry is.

One and a half months after the match against Everton we were all set to meet
United at home at Anfield. The clash had an added dimension for me. Riise against
Solskjær. The rivalry was perfect. Liverpool against Manchester United, me against
him. What had those journalists written? I was the new wine. Oh yes, I was on
top of the world, kind of like this: *Hello there at home, are you listening? It's time
for the changing of the guard. Just sit back and watch the match, then you'll see what
I mean. Are you listening? I'm going to be Norway's best football player of all time.*

We had kept winning after the victory at Goodison Park, we were above United
in the table and were brimming with confidence. Not only had we won the last
three matches against them, but in the previous week we had comfortably defeated
Charlton away, whereas United had scraped a draw against Leeds. Solskjær had

been introduced as a substitute and levelled the match in the final minute.

I had also arranged for loads of friends from Ålesund to come over for the match, seven or eight of them. They were all staying with me in Woolton. The day before the match I told them: 'I'm going to score.' They laughed. 'Wait and see.'

I was really fired up. I made a brash statement to the Norwegian newspapers, describing the amazing feeling of tackling and added that I was going to break David Beckham on my left side. It was blown all out of proportion in England with a very tabloid twist: 'I'll break his legs.' I remember waking up to the headlines. I ate breakfast and wondered what I'd done. I've always tried to create situations where I'm under pressure because I perform best like that, but this was maybe taking things a little too far. Most of all it was a little embarrassing. I was brand new in the Premier League and had a lot more than him to prove.

Before the match Phil Thompson said to me: 'Right, now you're really going to have to go out there and prove yourself.'

I went through the routine that I had decided to follow in the visiting dressing room at Goodison Park. I warmed up without shin guards and drank a Red Bull. I tightened my left shoe and ran out of the tunnel close to our captain. The rules state that he has to lead the team out on the pitch, but I wanted to be next in line behind him.

The atmosphere at Anfield was absolutely magical. We stood out there with our fans singing 'You'll Never Walk Alone' just like they always did. I went over to Beckham, apologised for the newspaper headlines and shook his hand. He smiled it off.

It was the middle of the day. A cold November day.

Manchester United took the kick-off and The Kop booed all of their players who touched the ball: Juan Sebastián Verón, Dennis Irwin, David Beckham, Ruud van Nistelrooy.

After half an hour, Michael Owen took advantage of a small slip-up by Wes Brown in United's defence to give us the lead with a lovely finish. Then, just a few minutes later, Graham Poll whistled for a shove in the back of Owen. The free-kick was to be taken from a distance, and from the side that was perfect for my left foot. We had agreed that I would take any free-kicks in that area, so even though I was new to the team, there was no discussion. My old teammate from Monaco,

Fabien Barthez, directed the wall. I heard him shouting. He hadn't been entirely convincing of late. Against us he had also fumbled a catch from one of my throw-ins. I placed the ball. I told Dietmar Hamann that I wanted him to roll the ball to my left, one-and-a-half to two yards, to get a better angle. 'Wait till I start my run-up.' He stood waiting. The referee adjusted the wall, which had crept closer again. This was a big chance for me; ever since the referee whistled for the foul I'd been thinking that. Now, now, now. They were singing my in the stands. I heard them. Thousands of voices. Then I took my run-up. Hamann rolled the ball away with the tip of his boot, a little harder than I had expected so I had to adjust my run. One of their players stormed towards me, Quinton Fortune, but I didn't care. I just thumped the ball, and I struck it cleaner than I had ever done before. It took off from my instep like a rocket. I struck it perfectly. I didn't even feel the ball. It hit the crossbar and landed behind Barthez, who had barely been able to register what happened. Afterwards I was told that the ball reached a speed of 112 kilometres per hour. From a distance of 26 yards. It was nine minutes past twelve in Liverpool. And once again they were singing my name on The Kop.

Joooooooooohn Arne Riise!
Oohh! Aaahhh!
I wanna know-ow-ow
How you scored that goal!

Beckham cut the deficit, then Owen scored one more and we ended up winning 3–1. That night Jamie Redknapp rang and said that all the lads were at The Living Room in Victoria Street. Even though my house was full of guests, I went to join them. I felt I had to, it would have been odd to turn down an invitation like that. When I walked through the door, the entire team got up and sang the same song that had been sung by the supporters earlier in the day. They had been drinking a little and were well under way, and they got the other guests in the bar to sing along. It was really touching. And embarrassing. I didn't drink, we had training the next day and I had people at home. It was just past midnight.

I scored against our two biggest rivals in my first autumn as a Liverpool player. Suddenly I was a real superstar. But I was a naive lad, I started to get a lot of friends, and it would turn out that not all of them were true friends. I couldn't tell them apart back then, I took what I could get. I wasn't fussy. I was walking on air. When a journalist asked me what I hoped to get out of my newfound status, I replied that I was hoping to get a chance to meet Britney Spears one day, and it came straight from the heart.

15

OLE GUNNAR SOLSKJÆR IS BELOVED IN NORWAY. HE IS NORWEGIAN IN the way we like. Humble in interviews. He never says anything wrong. He has always been portrayed as loyal and hard-working because he accepted sitting on the bench year in and year out at Manchester United. He started in the match against us in November 2001 but didn't make the most of his opportunity and was substituted for Dwight Yorke shortly after the interval. That's life sometimes. Solskjær was a so-called super-sub. Truth be told, he was given the chance to go to other clubs to get more playing time. Every time he said no. I've often wondered why. A friend of mine once wondered aloud if it was because as a striker at United, you had a lot more scoring chances every match. You are pretty much guaranteed to score plenty of goals, even as a substitute. As a regular on a weaker team, he would have had to show more.

I think my friend might have said that to make me happy. Because he knows that Solskjær is the only Norwegian footballer who has achieved anything close to what I have, yet Solskjær is the one who is loved for it in Norway, and that's something I've never quite got over.

Outside of Norway, my reputation is different. Ironically, it's more like Solskjær's. In England and Italy, the countries where I've spent most of my career, I think the vast majority of my teams' supporters would describe me as a hard-working, loyal, no-nonsense type of player. I hope they would say that I played with heart in every match, and that they think of me as a defender who had the ability to score spectacular goals in important matches.

But not in Norway. In Norway I was someone else.

Ole Gunnar would answer politely when journalists asked him something. He didn't do anything stupid. No Ferrari. No divorces. No text messages.

Yes, I've been a loudmouth, and I can say that it's because deep down I'm a fairly insecure guy, but it's probably not the sort of thing one should admit to. I've always been scared of not getting the honour I thought I deserved. I grew up in a family where we don't sit quietly hoping for something, we shout out loud to get what we think we deserve. All right, so I dyed my hair – that's the kind of thing the newspapers actually complained about at the time – but it was also because I had a redhead's complex. I turned up wearing yellow football boots, but if that's a crime, then I'm in very good company these days. I did a lot of stupid things, but can anyone claim that any of it was actually that bad? I didn't even get drunk aside from that one time. I was an ambitious defender, I was not a number 10, not a free spirit, not a dribbling genius. I was professional and serious. I worked hard and conscientiously, ran back and forth, up and down my left side. I had a cannon of a shot. Maybe my playing style didn't match my behaviour, the two didn't quite tally. Was that it? Or maybe people back home in Norway simply thought I was an idiot. That's their right. I couldn't even use alcohol as an excuse.

I considered drinking to be unprofessional for a footballer. Maybe it had something to do with my dad, my subconscious forcing me to stay away from it. I could drink when I retired, and I do have a drink or two now, but I prefer to be in control when I go out. There are too many people who like to make trouble when they see me. Obviously the majority of people are very nice, and I don't mind having my picture taken with people, not at all, but I often find that someone wants to have a row when I show up. That's why I always ring the restaurant before I go out. I ask for a table, then I have a chat with the doorman on the way in, so that he can keep a watchful eye, and I just give him a nod if I need help. What can I say? I wasn't exactly prepared that life was going to be like that when I decided to become a professional footballer. And that bothers me – probably far too much – that my reputation off the pitch in Norway so fundamentally distracts from my efforts as a football player.

I played 348 matches for Liverpool over the course of seven seasons, an average of nearly fifty per season. I earned myself a place on the list of fifty players with the most appearances in the club's history. After Liverpool I went to AS Roma and played with legends like Francesco Totti and Daniele De Rossi. I was managed by Claudio Ranieri, who called me the best left-back in Europe. And in 2010 when the *Liverpool Echo* asked readers to select the team of the decade, nearly ninety percent chose me as the top left-back. What else? Yes, I earned 110 caps for Norway, more than any other player.

Sorry for tooting my own horn, sometimes I get a little carried away. Ole Gunnar Solskjær would have kept quiet, and on occasion I wish I had that ability, but I don't. My family isn't like that. We say what we think, and we say it out loud. I have always said more than I should. I have all kinds of respect for Ole Gunnar Solskjær, he really was a super-sub with a practically God-given talent to pop up where he needed to be. And obviously we have one thing in common, we both won the Champions League. The one I was part of is called the Miracle of Istanbul. We haven't got to that part of the story yet. But it really was a miracle, and I was part of it.

16

JOHN CAREW AND I ARRIVED ON THE NORWEGIAN NATIONAL YOUTH scene around the same time, though he was a year older than me. I'm not a small guy, but he was huge, over 6ft 5in, weighing in at over fifteen stone. We got on well from the start. We both stood out a little. We weren't alike, but we weren't like the others either. He went to the big Spanish club Valencia when he was twenty, the summer prior to Liverpool buying me, at the same age. We used to send each other text messages after matches, nice comments, but also some sarcastic ones, of course. We maintained a kind of friendly rivalry. I liked John. He lived the jet-setting lifestyle, complete with cars and ladies. He performed at a level, which for a time, only I was able to match, and he did it so brilliantly, living life to the full, anything but the traditional, conscientious 24-hour Norwegian athlete.

17

GÉRARD HOULLIER WAS ALWAYS SWAGGERING AROUND IN A STYLISH coat and a red scarf, putting his arm around one of the players and saying a few well-chosen words. For me, and for many others, he was a father figure. That's why what happened was so shocking.

We prepared for the match as usual. We were facing Leeds at Anfield, and everyone reported to the hotel in the morning for breakfast and to find out the team selection and tactics. Houllier seemed fine. He was his normal self. In the first half he managed the team from the bench, and during the interval he calmly explained how we had to play to claw back Leeds' 1–0 lead.

I didn't see him keel over. I didn't even know he had. But after we left the dressing room, he told the other members of staff that he felt chest pains, and club doctor Mark Waller was summoned. Without those of us on the pitch realising it, he was driven to the hospital with sirens blaring. We were not told that his life was in danger until after the match. I didn't notice that he wasn't on the bench in the second half; like the rest of us, I was focused on the pitch. To learn that he underwent major heart surgery there and then, the thought of his wife and their two daughters, that scared me. Eleven hours in the operating room. He was only 54. Clearly it was going to be some time before he returned, *if* he returned. I remember him visiting us at the training ground one day. He had just popped in briefly, but straight away we could see how weak and poorly he was.

But in a way we were reinvigorated. We resolved to play for him, and just before Christmas we topped the league table. But then we started to struggle to win matches. We dropped down to fourth, though still only two points behind league leaders Arsenal by the new year.

When we travelled to Southampton in January, we had won only one of our previous six league matches. There was rain and fog like you only find in England. Just before we arrived at the stadium, I was told by Phil Thompson, who was managing the team in Houllier's absence: 'You've played twenty-seven matches in a row now. You need a rest.' I was left on the bench. With twenty minutes remaining in the match I was brought on. We were down 1–0 after a penalty, and the idea must have been that I was going to contribute with some offensive power, maybe exploit them with my long throw-ins towards the end of the match. Instead – after three minutes on the pitch – I scored an incredibly beautiful own goal, a header that went over Jerzy Dudek and into the far corner. With that I sealed Liverpool's first league loss away at Southampton in nearly eight years.

I was disappointed, but it wasn't too serious. I felt close to invincible after the goals I scored over my first autumn at the club. And four days later we were due to meet Arsenal at their home ground, Highbury. I lay awake in bed and thought about how I was bloody well going to show them. Own goal or not.

We were under siege. Freddie Ljungberg gave the home team a lead a quarter of an hour into the second half. Things were not looking bright for us at that point. We needed points in order to stay in contention for the title. Only minutes later we broke up another attack. I played the ball to Patrik Berger from the edge of our penalty box and continued up the left. Berger centred the ball to Steven Gerrard, who must have spotted my run out of the corner of his eye, because he laid on an absolutely beautiful pass that I received on the way to Arsenal's goal. I had run the length of the pitch. Suddenly I was alone with their keeper, and practically the only thing I could do was shoot the ball low and controlled inside the near post. It was that kind of season. I had scored against Everton, against Manchester United, against Newcastle, who were also fighting for top spot that year, and now I had scored against Arsenal.

In January, rumours started swirling again. Real Madrid were meant to be interested. It was suggested that I was going to replace Roberto Carlos. Hearing that was obviously pretty crazy, and big clubs are always on the look-out for young players who can perform at a high level. As flattered as I was, I had to keep reminding myself that everything in this business is a game. Huge sums of money and a lot of people who want it. Every agent has contacts with journalists. They dangle some bait for them and the papers blow things out of proportion. Even when it's unconfirmed speculation, they use it because it's juicy material. Rumours of interest from another club can force contract negotiations and wage increases, which the agent also earns from, obviously. I was not part of this game. I just wanted to say that. The only thing I wanted was to stay at Liverpool. I hoped the club knew that. Even though I was seriously flattered, I was also afraid that the manager would think I was after more money, or that I was ungrateful for what I had experienced. I didn't want to push. I heard players in the dressing room talk about how much they could make by demanding their image rights from the club, but that wasn't for me. Not that I think there was big money in it for someone with my looks, but I still thought it was disgusting. We made more than enough as it was, and you had to treat your club with due respect. However, I did get my first boot deal around that time. The others had probably been offered that kind of deal long before, but I was well pleased that Nike would supply me with as many boots as I wanted. In financial terms it wasn't much. But it was cool to have your own boot deal.

One UK rep came out to Melwood on a regular basis, bringing six or seven pairs of boots with him and we would have a chat about how things were going. I have always gone through a lot of boots, I need them to fit snug. For the most part I wear football boots that are at least one size too small so they feel close enough. It's incredibly painful, particularly when it's hot, and throughout my career I've had occasional issues with my toe nails falling out, but they have to be like that so I can hit my shots properly, feel my step, the push-off in the grass, the acceleration, and so I can get my timing right. They last only four or five matches, after that they've stretched too much. But maybe the coolest thing about the arrangement was that I could just ask for something and the factory made it. For example, they stitched Riise into them. I told them what I wanted and the next time the local rep brought the shoes to me exactly as I had requested. And that was life back then.

I had bags of fan mail delivered to me once a week. In the beginning I was determined to reply to all of them. The fans were extremely important to me. Obviously because they're the ones who come to the matches, but also in another way: I was obsessed with wanting them to like me, quite simply. I loved the attention. Even though I was quiet and shy as a child, I dreamed of being seen, being remembered and being famous. I'd had to grow up in a hurry but I was also very childish. I thought it was nice being recognised everywhere. Maybe they liked me a little more because I looked English. I always went to the back of the queue when we were going out somewhere, it wouldn't have occurred to me to do anything else, but then we were waved to the front. There wasn't a restaurant in Liverpool that wouldn't find me a table, even though I hadn't booked. I would ring and they'd take care of it. People from back home that I hadn't heard from in ages started to send text messages out of the blue, congratulating me on a victory, saying how they hoped to see me soon. I realise that above all, they wanted things from me, but deep down, it still made me happy.

Before our final match of the second group stage of the Champions League, at home against Roma, Gérard Houllier suddenly turned up at the team hotel. He had been away for five months. We hadn't been told anything in advance, and spontaneous cheers and applause broke out amongst the players. There he was again. He had been given the all clear during a holiday in France, he was just being cautious. Fired up, we beat Roma 2–0, something that earned us a quarter-final spot in the Champions League. There we defeated Bayer Leverkusen 1-0 at home in the first leg but lost the away match 4-2 and were eliminated.

Back home in England, we had reclaimed top spot with five matches remaining. In my first season at the club, we could win the league for the first time since the club's glory days of the 70s and 80s – the last title had come in 1990. However, Arsenal had two matches in hand, and no matter how much we hoped they would suffer a setback, it was no use. They would finish seven points ahead of us, and in the final match we had to beat Ipswich Town to secure second place ahead of Manchester United. Truth be told, Ipswich didn't offer much resistance, already prepared for relegation as they were. We played some beautiful football, and I scored the first two goals in what ended as a 5–0-victory.

I could not wait for the next season. Fortunately, I didn't know at the time that I was never going to come closer to winning the Premier League than during my debut campaign. Nor did I know what the Champions League was going to offer. Or that years later I was going to be responsible for one of the costliest and most spectacular own goals of the decade. I tried to adjust to life as a star. I didn't complain. But it was all very new, let's put it that way. Plenty of crazy stuff used to happen. One day I was told that someone famous and powerful wanted to meet Michel Owen and me. He wanted to have dinner with us.

'Okay?'

I don't think I was told his name at first, or else I just didn't catch it. It was Al-Saadi Gaddafi, son of the former Libyan dictator, Muammar Gaddafi. I was 21. I hadn't done anything other than play football. What were we going to talk about? Was I meant to prepare in some way? We met at a hotel near the airport. He rented an entire floor for one night. He arrived by private jet, was driven to the hotel in great haste, spent one night and then left. His trip there was secret. We had dinner surrounded by his security guards. They were everywhere, a lot of them. At first things went painfully slow. But then we were just sitting there: Michael Owen, me and Gaddafi's son. Then we started to talk about football training, and of course that's something I know about. He played himself, signed a contract with Serie A club Perugia that year, employing Diego Maradona as a technical consultant and Canadian sprinter Ben Johnson as his personal trainer. He only played one match as a substitute before he was caught for doping.

18

MY AGENT WAS EINAR BAARDSEN. WHY HIM, I CAN'T REALLY SAY. LIKE a lot of things in my life, it happened somewhat coincidentally. Although the way I trained and staked everything on my career was thorough and systematic, some of the decisions I made were to a large extent marked by chance and a lack of planning. Quite a lot of things have been decided in a hurry. Maybe it is due to how everything started with an unexpected phone call at a hotel in Hamar, how at first everything had to happen so quickly. When Monaco said they were interested, I was given just days to consider. I had no agent, I had my mum, and she asked for help from Gunnar-Martin Kjenner, who flew with us to Monte Carlo to help negotiate the Monaco contract. But he was just an advisor, not my agent. The fact that the choice happened to be Einar Baardsen was most of all down to a coincidental meeting at Theatercafeen in Oslo, as I recall. At the time, all I really wanted was to have an agent who was not my mum, so that Mum could just be Mum. That was in the autumn of 2000. Even though I was only twenty, things were different from when I was seventeen. I didn't want to have my mum with me everywhere I went: after all, I was living with someone, and I was going to be a dad.

Baardsen flew in from Stavanger and invited Mum to meet him at Theatercafeen, and maybe he had planned this all along, I don't know. In any case, the Norwegian TV star Dan Børge Akerø suddenly went over to their table and said that he knew and respected Baardsen's way of working. So Baardsen was our guy. He was the one who was with me at Jean Tigana's vineyard. The one who took the call from Liverpool.

Afterwards I found out that Akerø and Baardsen were childhood friends. And that they had bought a seaside hotel together outside Stavanger, and that Baardsen ended up in debt to Akerø, and that the hotel later went bankrupt. In fact, that was just the start.

19

IN MY FIRST SEASON AT LIVERPOOL, I WAS THE ONLY PLAYER TO APPEAR on the pitch in every league match. The club were pleased. When they offered to extend my contract until 2007, I accepted on the same day. That's how happy I was. The contract guaranteed me a minimum monthly wage of more than 1.5million kroner, around £200,000 today, net. There were also bonuses and potential private sponsorships. Over the summer holidays I proposed to Guri, who I had been with for three years at that point. When we were in Ålesund, I stayed with my parents and she and Ariana stayed with hers. Maybe it was a little odd, but that's what we did. Mum and Guri didn't particularly get on. So I proposed to her in the bedroom she grew up in. That *is* a little strange. Perhaps it was also an indication that we were still very young, despite everything. But it wasn't about common sense. I was practically overwhelmed by everything and excited about my life.

Before we returned to Liverpool, we had a big send-off in Ålesund with a hundred guests. I had made arrangements for a marquee right in the city centre. There I proposed to her for a second time, officially as it were, from the stage. I can see now that the whole thing had an air of being some kind of public display, with myself playing the role of the prodigal son.

As a player, you get a little nervous in the summer. Which players are coming in? Who do I have to compete with going forward? Saying that, I felt I was in a strong position after my first season. Gérard Houllier brought in El Hadji Diouf, Salif Diao and Bruno Cheyrou for a total of £18million. Diouf and Diao were coming off a brilliant World Cup campaign playing for Senegal, Diouf in particular having distinguished himself. Poor Bruno Cheyrou was singled out to be the new Zinedine Zidane, but of course there's nothing he could do about that. All three of them failed at Liverpool, Diouf's behaviour separated him from the others. He thought he was in a completely different league from the rest of us. His flashy clothes were a pitiful sight. He had a car, I don't even know what you'd call that colour. Diouf could have whatever car he wanted for my part, as long as he had trained hard and done the job he was extremely well-paid to do. He wasn't interested in anything but showing that he was something special. The only place he chose to not distinguish himself was on the pitch.

I preferred to concentrate on myself, working even harder than I did in the previous year. I believed I still had more to give, even though in August I was voted the year's best newcomer by *Match* magazine, ahead of Ruud van Nistelrooy. Leeds United manager David O'Leary also called me the best left-back in England.

I scored the only goal when we opened the league with a victory over Aston Villa at Villa Park. After seven matches, I was tied with Danny Murphy for top scorer on the team with three goals. At the beginning of November, we'd had the best start to a season in twelve years. Then things went south. First we lost to Middlesbrough, then we dropped out of the Champions League during the group stages, drawing 3–3 in the decisive match against Basel in November. We had already drawn with them at home in September. We'd needed a win to secure second place in the group behind John Carew's Valencia, and I was at fault for Basel's opening goal as we went 3-0 down. An eventual draw couldn't prevent us from being knocked out. Things really started to go wrong. We drew against Sunderland, lost to Fulham, whose home supporters peppered me with the usual disgruntled remarks because I had chosen Liverpool over them. In the following match we lost at home to Manchester United, and it continued like that. After a goalless draw against Everton three days before Christmas, we had only managed to scrape together two points out of a possible 21. We led against Arsenal two days before New Year's Eve, but then a penalty was given because I had supposedly tugged their winger by the jersey when he tried to race past me. I never did, but still it meant a yellow card and a spot-kick to Arsenal, safely converted by my former Monaco teammate, Thierry Henry.

Defeat at Newcastle and a draw with Aston Villa at the start of the new year completed an eleven-match winless sequence – the club's worst in the league since 1954. Another disappointment followed in March when we were knocked out of the UEFA Cup. We lost to Celtic in the quarter-finals. A 1–0 away defeat in

Glasgow was one thing. Far worse was losing 2–0 at home in the return leg at Anfield. We did not play well. The mood in the dressing room was not good after the final whistle. Two of the players were arguing. One berated the other for a stupid decision that spoiled a counter-attack. 'Shut up!' the other shouted back. 'Idiot!' Both were on their feet now. I'm not mentioning their names because you don't talk about what goes on in the dressing room. There's a code of honour in football. Anyway, it's not important, those kinds of things happened time and again. Someone flared up in disappointment, there was a lot at stake, and everyone always demanded the utmost of themselves and those around them. There was someone on hand to calm things down.

For me personally, my game wasn't bad at all. I enjoyed a lot of trust from Houllier and played more matches for Liverpool that year than Steven Gerrard and Jamie Carragher did: 56 to their 54 each. And when we played Arsenal at home at the end of January, I got my revenge for the incorrect penalty call at Highbury. With a rocket of a shot, impossible for David Seaman to stop, I cancelled out Arsenal's lead in a match that ended 2–2. When I scored against Middlesbrough in the middle of February, it was my seventh league goal of the season, incidentally the same number Ole Gunnar Solskjær scored as a striker for Manchester United.

After recovering a little towards the end of the season, we ended in fifth place, missing out on a Champions League spot after losing to Chelsea in the final match of the season. Obviously team results are what matter and we were hugely disappointed with our efforts, but the fact was that my own game hadn't been much worse than during my opening campaign'. During the season there had been rumours that Barcelona were interested in me, and that the club had made an offer of £6million, but I never heard anything concrete. Houllier had also been quoted in the papers saying that I was one of his most valuable players. All the same, there was nothing I wanted more than to remain at Liverpool. Loyalty, as I've mentioned before, was – and is – important to me.

I say that despite what I'm about to reveal.

20

ON 14 JUNE 2003 I MARRIED GURI AT BORGUND STAVE CHURCH, A beautiful medieval building. She was my first girlfriend. We'd been living together for four years and we had a beautiful daughter. The party was held at the Parken Hotel in Ålesund. There had been a lot of articles leading up to the wedding, about a guest list that included everyone from Al-Saadi Gaddafi to Prince Albert of Monaco. Two hundred and fifty guests had been invited. But if only the journalists had known. It was by the narrowest of margins that the entire wedding not was called off. I didn't want to get married. It's an awful thing to say, but it's the truth. I should not have proposed. I did it mostly because it seemed like the natural thing to do. That was the life I had imagined. I was going to get married, have children, settle down and buy a house. That was the kind of life you were supposed to have. So I proposed and then got on with planning the day: I booked the church then sorted the food, cake and rings. Invitations were posted. I don't know if panic was setting in, or if I just suddenly woke up and realised I didn't want to go through with it. That I had never wanted to. That I was too young. We were too young. Oh, God.

In the days leading up to the wedding, a series of crisis meetings were held, with her parents and me, with my parents, with counsellors, with agents. It was an insane commotion, obviously. I wanted to pull out, but it was too late. That was what they told me, and maybe they were right. Everyone had been invited. Everything was ready. The scandal would be too big. And we had a child together.

But wait. Is that the whole truth? That I got married to protect Ariana, to protect Guri? Can I really say that? My behaviour made the wedding a disaster for her. Without a doubt. She must have been terrified about what the future held for her.

Then why do it? I was a huge egotist. It's as simple as that. I made the easy choice. I did what I did so nobody would be disappointed. I was cowardly and immature. I thought, I might as well get married then get divorced in six months. I'm embarrassed about it, but that's what I thought. I have a wonderful daughter and I don't want to hurt her, but at the same time I want to tell it as it was. She deserves to know, and she's old enough now. In my defence, I would say that I was living in a bubble. I was a professional footballer playing for Liverpool. Above all else I was obsessed with doing well. Every single training session, every single match. Every day, every week for eleven months of the year. I could not let anything get in my way. All football players are egotists at this level. We forget everything around us, block it out. It's the only way to survive. I succeeded in doing that, too. I had had a thumping season before the proposal. Maybe I lost touch with reality. I was walking on air. I didn't think I could fail. I wanted a big celebration, maybe that was it. And what kind of party is better than a wedding? I was going to invite everyone, show my hometown how great I had become. That's the way I'm built: Look! Look at what I've accomplished!

And things got a little out of hand: I wanted to invite the Prince of Monaco; I did actually know him from when I lived there. I invited Al-Saadi Gaddafi, so he came with all of his bodyguards. I wanted to show everyone in the city who I was playing with: Steven Gerrard. Michael Owen. Jamie Carragher. I wanted to make people see that these were the kind of people that it was natural for me to invite. But I also knew these were also the guests who would quickly decline due to it falling in their own short holiday window, even though I did allow myself to hope. I knew my teammates wouldn't come. If you plan a wedding during the short period when they're on holiday, chances are good they'll be on the other side of the globe. Instead the papers wrote articles about all the people who didn't come. Who did I think I was?

Despite everything, it was a beautiful day. I held Ariana in my arms. I was 22 years old and I was rich. I now had an investment company in my name, Riise Invest, something Baardsen had set up. I dreamed of captaining the national team in a year or two. I knew the Prince of Monaco. I was friends with Steven Gerrard. I had everything to look forward to.

I looked out at all the wedding guests. A thought went out to my dad who wasn't there. I looked for Thormod but didn't spot him. My mum stood some distance away, speaking with someone whose back was turned to me. Nikola was sitting at a table with the old gang. Guri was chatting with some girlfriends.

I smiled at Ariana. I was scared.

21

RIGHT FROM THE START OF THE SEASON IN AUGUST 2003 SOMETHING was not quite right. There was a tension at the club after the poor results from the previous season, that was clear. But normally that sort of thing wouldn't rub off on me. I knew that I was strong, and my game had been good. Was it my private life that was getting in the way, an uncertainty at the choice I had made? In any case I was not my old self. Nor was Gérard Houllier, I would say. I stood behind him, as you do, but I began to sense a doubt as to whether he was the right man. But more importantly, I slowly got the feeling that he doubted himself. Maybe he had been weakened by his illness more than he cared to admit. He'd spent around half a billion kroner – worth over £70million in today's money – on new players, yet we still hadn't managed to become anything more than a nearly team.

None of the three players brought in the previous year had clicked. He had now picked up two new Frenchman who had been with Le Havre, Anthony Le Tallec and Florent Sinama-Pongolle. They were both promising players, but they didn't have the kind of stability in their game that was needed to lift the team. The Irish international, Steve Finnan, a 27-year-old from Fulham, proved to be the best purchase around that time, but with all due respect, not a purchase that would tip the league in our favour. By comparison, Chelsea, who had been taken over by Roman Abramovich that summer, bought thirteen players, including Claude Makélélé from Real Madrid, Hernán Crespo from Inter, Adrian Mutu from Parma and Juan Sebastián Verón from Manchester United, in addition to domestic players like Glen Johnson and Joe Cole from West Ham. They later added Scott Parker to their squad in the January transfer window.

I was one of the starting eleven when we played Chelsea at Anfield for the season opener. We lost 2–1. After a 0–0 draw in the next match away against Aston Villa,

I was left on the bench. I didn't play well that autumn. The confidence was gone. I no longer understood what Houllier wanted me to do. I was unclear when he wanted me to attack and when he wanted me to defend, and I lost the assuredness in my play, doubt seeped in, and I was caught out of position more and more often.

I always watched the matches on TV afterwards to learn from them, and this was a period when I saw myself do a lot stupid things on the pitch. I made stupid decisions. I can hardly think how stupid it must have looked to the fans. I was passive and lacked confidence in most of what I did.

Guri and I tried to work things out as best we could. We arranged for a babysitter and went out, just the two of us, in an effort to be boyfriend and girlfriend. The sitter's name was Michelle, and her boyfriend Lee was such a massive Everton supporter that he refused to come to our house. He didn't want to be seen with me. One-and-a-half years it took. I remember coming home one evening and Michelle was sitting on the sofa. I asked for her boyfriend's number. Then I texted him: 'Fancy a game of pool?' Then he came slinking over.

We became friends after that. But he still didn't want to be seen with me.

Against Tottenham I didn't play at all, and against Everton on 31 August I came on with a minute left to play. It was a fantastic and badly needed 3–0 victory, but I was not a significant participant. Quite simply, I felt left out.

Then I travelled to Norway. The national team was meeting Bosnia-Herzegovina in a qualifying match for Euro 2004. I sat on the plane, looked down at the black September sea. I didn't know if I'd get a chance to see my mum while I was in Norway, but a meeting with Einar Baardsen was always on the cards. At the time I considered him one of my closest friends.

22

THE PRESS DUBBED IT 'THE BATTLE OF DRAMMEN'. ON MONDAY 1 September 2003, the squad for the European Championship qualification match against Bosnia-Herzegovina was selected. The match was crucial if we were to reach the finals in Portugal. We had to play in Bosnia on Saturday 6 September, and the squad met in Oslo on Tuesday. The journalists wanted to know if I thought it was a disadvantage that I had received less playing time at Liverpool early in the season, and even though I replied that it was an advantage to be rested, that was not the whole truth. The papers followed the training session and rated how they thought we had done. Everyone scored rather low, I got a two out of six, which hadn't exactly helped. But I trained hard, on my own as well as in the team training session. After the others left, I stayed behind practising corners. Corner after corner, in an attempt to get them the way I wanted them, hard and accurate.

We lost the match 1–0. The home crowd threw bottles and lighters at me when I took throw-ins, and the newspapers were merciless afterwards, that's how they were when things didn't go well. My attitude was described as unacceptable. It was claimed that as one of the big names on the national team, I should be embarrassed, that I seemed disinterested and weak in the challenges. And maybe that was true. In any case, I was piss-poor. I didn't sleep, and then we went home. Sitting at the back of the plane were the journalists who had written crap about us.

On Monday we had a training session at Marienlyst Stadion in Drammen in advance of the international friendly against the European Championship hosts Portugal two days later. We warmed up for a while, and I saw John Carew standing a little way off, on his mobile. Obviously that was completely off limits, and he wouldn't have done it unless it was important. I didn't hear what he said, but I know that this was around the time when John found out that he was going to be a dad after a one-night-stand, and that he had demanded a paternity test. He was under enormous pressure. But we weren't on bad terms.

After the warm-up we practised attack sequences. On one of the attempts I chose to shoot instead of centring to John. He got furious and started shouting at me, I don't remember what he said. It's not important, and I can't remember what I shouted back either. We simply argued about the choice I had made. We probably accused each other of being selfish, and that was immature and true of both of us. We clashed in the heat of the moment, but that happens all the time in training sessions, and Steffen Iversen was quickly over to get between us, trying to make some sarcastic comment to disarm the situation, which didn't exactly calm our tempers in the way that he had imagined. I remember John saying: 'Just wait till we get on the bus.' We weren't going to argue in front of the journalists. And I must have replied along the lines of, 'Yeah, bring it on,' and when we jogged off afterwards, I was running next to John and spat in front of his shoes. What can I say? It's embarrassing. I really tried to provoke him. We knew each other really well by then, so I must have known which buttons to push.

We had kept the argument going for nearly two hours by the time we boarded the bus. I was two seats ahead of him, near the back of the bus.

'I didn't do anything wrong by shooting.'

'Shut it,' he said.

'Idiot,' I said.

'Shut it,' he replied.

'Idiot.'

'Shut it.'

I remember we were standing now, both of us. I wondered why John was holding a shoe with his huge fist wrapped around it. 'Are you going to hit me with your shoe? Hit me then!'

But then we sat down. I picked up my mobile and was fiddling with it. I thought we were finished. When the training session was over, you let it go. Whatever happens there, stays there.

Then I was suddenly felt a hard blow from his fist against my temple. I had no chance to protect myself. The blow came from behind, struck cleanly, and my head pounded against the side window before slumping forward on the head rest. But he was bent over the seat and continued to pound me, now with his elbow, with everything he could muster, until the others managed to tear him away and draw the curtains. I was out cold. The guys later told me that my head had been hanging limply by the aisle. John was ordered to the front of the bus by the team doctor while I sat on the floor. My jaw and temple were swelling up in a hurry and the doctor examined me. I was probably more shocked at what had happened than anything.

That night it was clear that John was going to be sent home. Anything else would have been ridiculous. He had crossed the line. But I went up to his hotel room when I found out. I knocked on the door. I liked the guy. I wish I'd known what he was struggling with, and that he had known more about the kind of problems I was having. But nobody talked about those sort of things on the national team. It's not the place to air your personal problems.

John let me in his room. For nearly an hour we sat talking, but nothing too serious. We kept it superficial and cheeky, maybe that was all we could manage.

True, I wanted to be the biggest star on the national team, but we were such different players. There was room for both of us. I sincerely thought that the more of us who did well the better. We weren't a big country. More than anything, I wanted to play in a major tournament for Norway. I wanted him back as soon as possible. I knew that he was mentally strong, so I wasn't worried about him. But I was worried about the national team without him.

At half seven the next morning I was examined at the Oral and Maxillofacial Surgery department at Ullevål hospital. They said that I'd been lucky. It could have been far worse.

That day the incident travelled around the world. I was ashamed, but also unsettled. Instead of seeing a 22-year-old and a 23-year-old who were both struggling with things in their personal lives, everyone saw two pampered footballers who didn't know how to behave. There may have been some truth in that but there was a lot more to it. I've later thought that even though I was the one who got knocked out, the incident seemed to cast a darker shadow on me. As though it showed me as being weak, as an unbearable, snotty brat who was finally put in his place. Not that they defended the method that was used, and of course John also paid his penalty. He was sent home, while I practically managed to wriggle my way out of it. I don't know if I'll ever manage to escape that image here in Norway, though.

Damn, I regret everything that happened that day.

23

MY THIRD YEAR IN LIVERPOOL WAS DIFFICULT.

I was in a marriage I didn't want to be in. I was a newlywed, but there was no love between us. I felt like everything we did was playing for the gallery. I wanted a divorce, but at the same time I was terrified at the thought of a life without Ariana.

My game wasn't functioning either. I drifted in and out of the team, but the entire squad was struggling. Between September and October we lost against Charlton, Arsenal and Portsmouth in three successive league matches. John Carew opted not to return to the national team. I tried to make up for everything that had happened by pushing myself harder than I thought possible, and we managed to scrape past Romania and take second place. We were equal on points, and they had a better goal difference, but in our two head-to-head clashes, we had a win and a draw. It couldn't get any closer than that, but we were given the chance to play two play-off matches in a final attempt to reach the European Championship in the summer. While fortune had been on our side during qualification, it certainly wasn't when our opponent was drawn. We were to play two matches against Spain of all teams, in November 2003. Once again there were rumours that Barcelona were looking at me. Miraculously we suffered only a narrow 2-1 loss in Madrid, largely thanks to phenomenal goalkeeping from our keeper, Espen Johnsen. I had a poor match, which strictly speaking was in keeping with my form. At Ullevaal we were going to take advantage of the time of year. That was the plan. The weather was cold and Nordic, the pitch looked like a farmer's field, and this was intended to spoil the Spaniards' tiki-taka game. What can I say? We were outplayed, beaten 3-0. We got a lesson in how football should be played. Claus Lundekvam was our captain. John Carew still wasn't selected. He had actually sent a letter to the football association stating that he could help out during the play-off matches and make a special appearance for the national team, but nothing came of it.

I returned to Liverpool. I was going to concentrate fully and completely on club football. But things never really got on track. In the beginning of December we were knocked out of the League Cup by Bolton in front of our home fans. In the FA Cup we couldn't get past Portsmouth. We still hadn't made it to the middle of December when we lost to Southampton at home in the league. Our loyal audience whistled at us, and who could blame them. We were terrible. Gérard Houllier was singled out by the bookies to be the first manager sacked in the Premier League. That poison in sport called doubt spread through the team. It seeped into everything. It seemed like Houllier began to doubt his own system and what he stood for. In the end hardly anything seemed to work.

For the first time in my career I began to struggle with minor injuries. First a bad ankle, then a double pulled groin. My play was ineffective. I could understand Houllier leaving me out of the squad. The only thing I could do was train hard and hope that I'd rediscover my form. At our home in Woolton, Guri and I lived in a kind of exhausting silence. Ariana was the light that I clung to. A three-year-old girl whom I spent most of my time with, and who gave me more comfort than anyone.

Over the course of the season I slowly fought my way back into the squad. I started the final eight league matches. In the end we managed to secure fourth place and therefore a spot in the Champions League qualifying rounds.

I remember sitting at home watching the final at the end of May that year. My old club, Monaco, had made it all the way there. They had knocked out Real Madrid in the quarter-final and Chelsea in the semi-final. It was a stunning achievement. I was a little divided. Of course I'd left them to come to a bigger club, but I was happy for Monaco. They had given me my first chance, and I'm still recognised by people working in the local restaurants I used to go to. But obviously it was a little annoying, not least because everyone always reminds me about it. That was where *you* played.

Monaco met Porto, led by a lesser known manager at the time: José Mourinho. They had nearly been knocked out by Manchester United, but my old friend Costinha from my time in Monte Carlo had scored in injury time at Old Trafford to secure a surprising place in the quarter-finals.

For the better part of half an hour the match stayed level but then Mourinho's

Porto took over. In the second half there was only one team on the pitch. It ended 3–0.

I picked up Ariana. Next year's final was going to be played in Istanbul.

24

WHEN WE FLEW TO AWAY MATCHES WITH THE NATIONAL TEAM, we always travelled on the same plane as the journalists. We always sat at the front of the plane, they sat at the back. And then they started to order drinks. That was the norm. Same story the following day. We trained early in the morning. They followed the training session, wrote brief reports for the newspaper, and then they would look for a bar, which they invariably found. That was clear from the smell. When they interviewed us they stunk of booze. They didn't look good. Hair all over the place. Stained shirts. Exhausted after too much partying and too little sleep, but if they got word that any of us had been out having a beer, they wrote indignantly back home about the unprofessional behaviour that required consequences from the management of the national team. Then they watched the match, perhaps butchered us. We read what they wrote. Every player does. Some take it more personally than others, like me, even though I knew I shouldn't. And on the way home, while we read what they had written, they sat at the back of the plane, drinking and hollering.

25

THE SUMMER OF 2004 WAS CHAOTIC. AFTER SIX YEARS AT THE CLUB, Gérard Houllier left at the end of May. I don't know if he got the sack, or if he just felt that it was time to resign. Regardless I think it was a sensible decision.

The papers were filled with stories about how Steven Gerrard was considering leaving the club. It was true. He was not pleased with the state of affairs at Liverpool — who would be after the season we'd just had? Chelsea were one of the clubs attempting to lure him away. With Roman Abramovich's millions and José Mourinho's recent appointment as manager, they offered huge sums of money and greater opportunities to win trophies, and he was close to leaving. Extremely close. The contract negotiations were more or less complete, as I understood it. At least the personal terms. He'd decided to leave. But he was under intense pressure. I sensed that it was hard on him. Liverpool was his hometown, he'd been a Liverpool player all his life and had a great passion for the fans and the club.

There was also talk that Michael Owen was on his way out and even though we didn't know how it was going to turn out, an uncomfortable feeling that things were in danger of falling apart began to seep in: Gerrard was our captain and Owen was our top scorer. At the same time my marriage was close to dissolving. It affected me. I had a three-and-a-half year old daughter, and the mere thought of her not being there when I came home was unbearable. Every day I dropped her off at nursery before training, and it was my job to pick her up as well. I loved doing it. I remember all the times she spotted me and came running towards me the way little kids do, the way she shouted 'Pappa' with that tiny little voice of hers.

In the end Gerrard decided to remain. One condition he received from the management was a promise of continued investment in the team, but he also had good people around him who gave him good advice. If he had left, it would have been a disaster for the team but probably for him as well. He would have hurt his reputation in his hometown. I think it could have got downright nasty.

Rafael Benítez was announced as our new manager in the middle of June. He came to the club after leading Valencia to La Liga and UEFA Cup glory in the 2003/04 campaign. It was the second time in three years Valencia had won the league under his stewardship. It was some achievement to repeat the trick, finishing ahead of both Real Madrid and Barcelona. The European Championship had just started in Portugal. As usual I followed the tournament from the comfort of my sofa, and God, what a miserable tournament it was. Otto Rehhagel's Greece bored their opponents to death and won.

With the appointment of a new manager, obviously the level of optimism grows, as well as a little fear. There's no point denying it. *When's he going to put his mark on the team, clear the ranks, buy new players? Will he use me? What does he know about me? Which system is he going to use?* And it wasn't as though I was in the form of my life when Benítez took over. For the first time at Liverpool I had experienced proper adversity; I had no reason to feel comfortable. Benítez sold a number of players and he began to sign others from his homeland, including Xabi Alonso, Josemi and Luis García. Just as my teammates had observed me when I arrived, I did the same with the new signings. For the most part it was quick to see who would manage and who would fade away. There were undoubtedly some world-class players, particularly García and Alonso. In his first match, it took Xabi 35 minutes before he failed to complete a pass.

I remember the meeting when Benítez introduced his playing philosophy to us. He told us that he loved hard-working players, team players who never gave anything less than their full effort, who dug deep in every match. In addition he said that his tactical plans depended on players who could master several positions on the pitch and could run a lot. I sensed that I could get a bigger role at Liverpool. Everything was set. I viewed it as a fresh opportunity. A clean sheet.

Whereas Houllier was a manager who would put his arm around you and be a kind of father figure, Benítez was primarily a hard-nosed tactician. He made it perfectly clear to us: all eleven players have to know their positions, where to run, and what to do on the pitch at all times.

The change suited me well. My confidence returned. I switched from number 18 to number 6 after Markus Babbel went to Stuttgart; I still preferred having an old-fashioned squad number from the starting eleven. I asked Benítez and he agreed to it. It felt good. I trained harder than ever. I had to show my best side for the new manager. Benítez was not generous with compliments, it wasn't his style. He made us crave them. It bothered other players more than me. I was used to it from managers.

Matters at home were becoming very clear: we had to get a divorce. Not that we really argued or anything, but it was as though everything was dead, and that was not the kind of life for either of us.

I blocked out these thoughts, worked hard at training sessions, and when the matches started, I went on the pitch and got down to business. During the 2004/05 pre-season I scored one of the most beautiful goals of my career. In one of the summer build-up matches – against Celtic, the team that had knocked us out of the UEFA Cup in 2003 – I hammered in the opening goal from 35 yards after four minutes of play. I was back. Twenty minutes later I lobbed the ball ahead to Michael Owen, who made it 2–0. The game ended 5–1.

Two weeks later – on 10 August – we played our first important match of the season. It was the first of two games against the Austrian club Grazer AK to qualify for the group stage of the Champions League. Already Benítez's brand of football could be seen in our play. There were fewer long passes and the classic passing game of Liverpool was back. The first fixture was played at the harmoniously named Arnold Schwarzenegger Stadion. Gerrard scored two in a comfortable and unremarkable 2–0 win. More remarkable was that Michael Owen was left on the bench and didn't appear. Speculation was rampant. Had he been brought on as a substitute, the rules dictated that he not could play for any other club in the Champions League that season. And only three days later the shocking news was announced to our fans: Michael Owen had been sold to Real Madrid. I wasn't that shocked. He was a fantastic player, he could score goals just for the fun of it, but my impression was that he was no longer wanted by the club.

However, there was other news that weighed on me. The papers had caught wind that Guri and I were getting a divorce. They posted pictures from our wedding: I was 23 years old, already divorced, and father of a young child. I stood outside the house when Guri and Ariana left. A neighbour drove them to the airport. I stood there crying when the car was gone. When I went back inside, the only thing in the house I could look at were pictures of Ariana. Photographs from her nursery, her on a blanket in the park, smiling and laughing. I saw her little Liverpool kit lying on the bed.

The next day we played the return match against Graz at Anfield. We did just enough to progress, and barely that, some might say. But I thought of the gossip mags, the fucking journalists who kept ringing and harassing the mother of my daughter, and I played with all my heart, running up and down the wing like never before. We lost 1–0 but went through 2–1 on aggregate. At night I lay awake after the match. One thing was clear to me in the dark: I was returning to form after a poor season. I wasn't going to let problems in my personal life affect my performance. I was stronger than that.

26

AROUND THE SAME TIME MICHAEL OWEN LEFT THE CLUB, DANNY Murphy also went. The two of them were best mates with Jamie Carragher and Steven Gerrard. Carra and Michael were a double act, as were Stevie and Danny, and the four of them were often seen hanging out together. Now two of them had been sold. In professional football, there's little you can do about it. Friendships get broken up. Danny was a close friend of mine, too, and I depended on him. Danny, Stevie, Michael, Carra and I, along with Didi Hamann, were a close-knit group at the club.

Following the transfers, Carragher and Gerrard stepped forward as the clear leaders of the squad. Carragher was an Everton supporter, a bluenose, born in Bootle, while Gerrard was from Huyton. The two of them now stuck together, always sitting next to each other on the team bus, sharing a room at the hotel. To me they represented everything that was good about the club that I was so proud to play for. Their roots in the city ran deep and they wanted to contribute to the local community that had nurtured them. Obviously, I was no Scouser – even though I might look a bit like one – but these were values I was personally drawn to. I disliked how football was becoming largely about money. Football was meant to make people happy, it was for the fans. We were no billionaire's plaything, not financed by a Russian oligarch, we were Liverpool. It was supposed to be about heart, not greed and ego.

Carragher and Gerrard, like me, were obsessed by football. They had played and played and played during their entire childhood, and it continued to be the one thing they wanted to do more than anything. I remember many years later Gerrard telling me that his best memory as a footballer was back when he was an apprentice at Melwood, where at the age of sixteen he cleaned floors and boots and pumped up balls and played football without having to concern himself with anything else. I get what he meant, though I'm sure a lot of things in life would have been easier with more ample means.

I wanted to live up to the legacy of Liverpool teams of the past. I wanted to make our fantastic supporters proud. I wanted to learn from Carragher and Gerrard. I soaked up everything. Carra was clever and witty, Stevie more reflective and withdrawn. But both of them – just like me – were pathologically obsessed with winning, though Carragher was probably worse than Gerrard. Carra had no qualms about cheating to win a game of five-a-side during training sessions. He also became the main cog in our defence over the years, the brains and driving force from centre-back. Both Carragher and Gerrard represented a thing that appealed to the depths of my soul: fight to the bitter end. They never let up. They waged war with sliding tackles and crunching challenges, not even letting up when cramp set in. Carragher broke his leg against Blackburn Rovers without realising it and insisted he could walk it off.

The start to our league campaign in 2004 was not bad but when we lost 2–1 to Manchester United at Old Trafford in late September, we were nine points back from the leaders, Arsenal. This would eventually turn out to be Chelsea's year in the Premier League. We dropped all six points against them in the league at Stamford Bridge and at Anfield. Chelsea lost just one match that entire Premier League season, giving up just fifteen goals. As a team, we weren't able to perform consistently, finishing 37 points behind them in fifth. But my game was better than ever, I have to say. I was back. I missed my daughter. I had her name tattooed on my forearm and I played for her, or for us, maybe.

My self-confidence blossomed under Rafael Benítez. He trusted me and once again I became one of the key players at the club. My old childhood friend, Nikola, had moved in with me. I had spent six months traipsing alone around the house before I finally got in touch with him. Nikola didn't hesitate when I rang him up. 'I'm booking the ticket!' I shouted into the phone.

I scored against Charlton when we beat them 2–0 at the end of October, and it was as though something inside me loosened up. I hadn't scored in 83 consecutive matches, but then I notched my second the following week against Blackburn, and it wasn't long before I had the opportunity to beat my record of seven league goals achieved during my first season. I played match after match after match. Never substituted. My game was on track. In December 2004 almost everything I attempted on the pitch succeeded. In the Christmas and New Year's fixtures

I scored three and assisted a further three. Still we were lagging behind in the table. We weren't functioning in the league. The distance to the top teams increased. There was an imminent danger that we wouldn't finish in the top four, which would exclude us from the Champions League the following season.

In late February 2005 we met Chelsea for the third time that season. It was an important match for us, the final of the League Cup at the Millennium Stadium in Cardiff. A chance to win a trophy and get a little breathing space in what was proving a difficult season. The match had hardly started when Fernando Morientes hit a cross. I saw the ball coming towards me – it was almost as though I was in a silent film, watching it move closer. I took aim with my left foot. I didn't want to bring the ball down, I didn't want to wait for anything, I just hit it with everything I could muster as soon as the ball was low enough to volley. I struck it perfectly. Petr Čech didn't have a chance to react. We were ahead after just 45 seconds. The TV commentator said that the stupidest thing Chelsea could have done was let a ball like that fall to my left foot. He mentioned that I had plenty of time to get nervous as the ball approached but it was a safe bet that I wouldn't. He was right. My teammates stormed towards me. Steven Gerrard, making his first appearance in a cup final as captain, simply repeated: 'Ridiculous! Ridiculous!'

It was my eighth goal of the season and a new record for me at Liverpool.

For nearly eighty minutes it looked as though we were going to be able to lift the cup and finally have cause to celebrate, but then Gerrard got unlucky defending a free-kick from Paulo Ferreira. He tried to nod the ball away for a corner but instead the ball curled into our own net. The match went into extra time; Gerrard urged us on but I could see that he was really bothered by his own goal. In the end we lost 3–2. We lay exhausted on the grass afterwards, and I remember José Mourinho walking around trying to console us. He had been ordered to the stands by the referee during the match, after gesturing to our fans with a finger to his lips, shushing them, but it was big of him to think about us in the midst of their victory celebration. 'Well played,' he said.

In the Champions League that year we had been drawn in a group with Olympiacos, Deportivo La Coruña and my former club, Monaco. Even though these were strong teams, it was a winnable group. But our play was less than convincing. Prior to the final round of matches of the group stage, we were three points behind

Olympiacos and two behind Monaco for the second-place finish that was needed to advance to the round of 16. The pressure on us was enormous before the decisive match on 8 December, at home at Anfield. We had to win. 1–0 would be enough, but if Olympiacos scored, we had to score two goals more than them.

We opened strongly but it soon became clear that Rivaldo harboured sinister plans. The Brazilian, who only a few years earlier had been one of the top players in the world at Barcelona, was out for revenge. The previous season he had struggled at AC Milan, and in an interview he had said that it was his dream to conclude his career at Liverpool, but Houllier had simply brushed the prospect aside. Now he dribbled circles round us in his solo raids on our defence. In the end Sami Hyypiä had to bring him down, and Rivaldo placed the ball to take the free-kick. Twenty-six minutes had elapsed. We had six men in the wall and our keeper, Chris Kirkland, screamed at us to stand closer. Rivaldo stood completely still. He took two steps back. Then he sent the ball over the wall and into the net with his left foot. Kirkland was furious, while Gerrard shouted at him for being out of position. In frustration, Gerrard kicked the ball away and was shown a yellow card, meaning he wouldn't play the following match. Now we had to score three goals to advance.

As usual Benítez was the epitome of calm in the interval. He put some simple tactical changes on the board. We switched to three at the back. Djimi Traoré was substituted for Florent Sinama-Pongolle. A defender out and a forward in: 'Be brave. We have one more half to stay in Europe. Go out and show me how much you want it. Go out and show our supporters.'

Only two minutes in, Harry Kewell ran down the left wing and managed to cross the ball. In front of goal and fresh off the substitutes' bench, Sinama-Pongolle appeared and tapped the ball over the line, then ran to collect it as quickly as possible for the restart. Benítez just took a quiet glance at his watch. But the roar from the crowd was fierce. They were in a frenzy.

First and foremost the second half belonged to Steven Gerrard. He fought like a tiger, he was everywhere, driving us forward. But we were struggling to find a goal. When we finally made it 2–1, only ten minutes remained. Benítez glanced at his watch again as we celebrated on the way back to the halfway line. We needed one more goal. Anfield was rocking. I remember Gerrard shouting something at us but I couldn't hear anything above the din. I assumed he was saying the same thing

Carragher was hollering at us – keep calm. But with only four minutes remaining, Carra himself went on the attack. He dribbled his way forward. It was an extremely unusual sight. To hell with calm. If something didn't happen soon, our European adventure would be over within minutes. I had to smile when Carra suddenly made a Cruyff turn by drawing the ball back and spinning 180 degrees to enter Olympiacos' penalty area. He kicked the ball neatly to Neil Mellor. Mellor rose into the air and I could hear Gerrard shouting for it. Mellor must have heard him because he cushioned a header back to Gerrard. The ball bounced once. It was not an easy ball. But Gerrard was unstoppable in the second half. He hammered the ball with a straight instep from 25 yards. It was so beautiful. A half-volley to make it 3–1. We advanced having scored all our goals in the second half. The fans were hysterical. Gerrard pumped his fists and we chased after him. Everyone in the stands was on their feet screaming. It was a feverish Wednesday night. Only Benítez stayed calm.

One thought stuck with me in the dressing room afterwards because what we had experienced was so extreme: Maybe this is our year?

My play had been noticed. In January 2005, Inter Milan rang my agent. Roberto Mancini had taken over the team that summer and he wanted me at the San Siro to strengthen the squad. But I wasn't interested – I had other things to concentrate on.

We drew Bayer Leverkusen in the round of 16. The first match was played at Anfield, and my game continued to function well. I scored the second goal from a free-kick, and was given a standing ovation when I was substituted with one minute remaining and a 3–0 lead. Unfortunately Jerzy Dudek made a terrible blunder and Bayer Leverkusen cut the lead to 3–1 with the final kick of the match. Usually that kind of miss at the end of a game wouldn't matter, but now it created needless tension ahead of the return clash. With an away goal secured, the Germans could advance with a 2–0 home win at the BayArena, and this was the team that had defeated Real Madrid, Roma and Dynamo Kyiv at home in the group stage.

Two weeks later we travelled to Leverkusen. We disproved all the predictions that we would lose to a strong Leverkusen team on home soil. We played an absolutely brilliant match. Once again we won 3–1 and advanced to the quarter-finals of the Champions League with a whopping 6–2 victory on aggregate. There we faced Zlatan Ibrahimović's Juventus. The prelude to that match centred around the gruesome happenings the last time these two clubs had met: the tragedy at the Heysel Stadium in Brussels twenty years earlier.

The first match was played at Anfield on 5 April, and though we couldn't dwell on the backdrop to the game, we could sense the mutual respect when fans from both teams held a banner together, bearing the message 'Memory and Friendship' down on the pitch before kick-off. Spurred on by the sense of occasion, we dominated the match and led 2–0 at the break. Unfortunately, they got a lucky goal past our nineteen-year-old reserve keeper, Scott Carson, who was making his Champions League debut. Luckily it didn't end up hurting us. Playing at home at the Stadio Delle Alpi in Turin the following week, Juventus were strangely tame. Fabio Cannavaro had a header ring off the post early on, but otherwise we had little problem holding them to a goalless draw. We were through to the semi-final of the Champions League. Our fans were in ecstasy, just as we were. The final match had above all been a defensive achievement, nonetheless, we were nearing a final in the Champions League. Both the club and the supporters had missed big victories. All of 21 years had passed since Liverpool's last triumph in the most distinguished of all European tournaments. In 1984 the Champions League was still known as the European Cup, and the heroes of Liverpool back then were players like Kenny Dalglish, Bruce Grobbelaar, Graeme Souness, Ian Rush and – at left-back – Alan Kennedy. This team had faced Roma, who had the Brazilian legend Falcão playing in midfield. The final went to penalties that year, and it was Kennedy who put away the winner, when sending Roma's keeper, Franco Tancredi, the wrong way. But that was a long time ago.

We poured into the visiting dressing room in Turin, shouting and screaming. *Fucking brilliant! Awesome!* We thumped one another on the back. Eventually I sat down on the bench and as usual I couldn't wait to get my tight shoes off. My toes ached, and they continued to hurt as I sat in stockinged feet. I unwound the tape. I pulled my sweat-drenched jersey over my head and leaned back with a towel around my neck.

Alan Kennedy had struck the decisive penalty in 1984. He had scored the winner in the 1981 European Cup final too. Everyone remembered him. Now I was playing left-back for Liverpool. Now it was my turn to do something I'd always be remembered for.

27

I HAD TO ASK BENÍTEZ FOR SOME TIME OFF. ON 16 APRIL, AFTER THE league match against Tottenham at Anfield, I went directly to the airport where a private jet awaited me. It was to attend the official opening of Aalesund's new stadium. The shipping magnate Olav Nils Sunde had placed his aeroplane at my disposal. He had personally contributed £5million towards the financing but he noted during his speech that my sale to Monaco, as well as previous contributions from the Norwegian-American Reidar Tryggestad, had made the construction of the new stadium possible. 'They brought in money for the club when it was virtually on its back, broken,' he said.

I looked forward to watching Aalesund play. I followed them closely from England. They were still my club. 'Their coach Ivar Morten Nordmark' had returned them to the Tippeligaen, and that night they were set to face Odds BK at the new ground.

I'd had some good chats with Olav Nils Sunde about the statue he wanted erected outside the stadium. 'We want to honour you,' he had said, and I was incredibly moved. I thought that it would be the perfect middle finger to those who had bullied me.

Not everyone agreed with his decision. Nordmark was insistent that it not be named after me. He had even put his position at the club on the line for it. Nordmark had no doubt made a substantial contribution to the club. He'd told the lads in the dressing room that he would step down as manager of the club if the statue was named 'John Arne Riise'. All I can say is that it makes me sad to hear that he would say that.

I was picked up at Ålesund Airport and driven into town. My flight had arrived late and I only caught the final eight minutes at the Color Line Stadion but they were the minutes to catch. Aalesund went from 1–0 down to 2–1 up as I watched.

After the match I was shown the statue. It was over eight feet high and made of bronze, and there was no doubt that it depicted me. But where they had said there would be a plaque reading 'John Arne Riise', it read 'The football player'. I was proud nonetheless. I mean, I was 24 years old and had a statue of me kicking a ball with my left foot outside the city's new football stadium.

It remains there.

28

THE SEMI-FINAL OF THE CHAMPIONS LEAGUE WAS THE ONLY THING
on our minds. The league was winding to a conclusion. We had a unique opportunity
to make history. It felt like the entire city was buzzing during the preceding weeks.
AC Milan and PSV Eindhoven had been drawn to face each other in the other semi-
final. We were going to meet Chelsea for the fourth and fifth time that season.
The first three we had lost. We were more than thirty points behind them in the
league. Chelsea were huge favourites but we weren't bothered by it. There was no
way we were going to lose two matches to the rich man's club from London.
The first match was at Stamford Bridge, the return at Anfield. I prepared by
watching videos of old matches. In that way I can be precise and methodical. I wasn't
nervous. I knew what was required of me. I was going to deliver. Benítez was clear
in the preparations, in the away match we had to show the same defensive strength
as in the quarter-final against Juventus. We had to focus on keeping a clean sheet.
If Chelsea didn't score at home, our prospects would be good for the following
week when they had to enter our fortress, with our extremely loyal and extremely
loud fans.

My performances had been good. I'd assisted on both goals when we defeated
Portsmouth a week before in the first leg. The night before we left, I sensed a kind
of calmness. I played pool with Nikola. And during the warm-up on the pitch I felt
the same thing, tranquillity.

We were under pressure from the start of the match but I did get an opportunity,
which Petr Čech just managed to get his gloves on my effort. It ended 0–0 in London,
something we were obviously extremely pleased with.

When we played evening matches in the Champions League we stayed at a hotel the night before, even when we were at home. Before the second leg against Chelsea the squad met up at the Radisson Blu Hotel. The ferry terminal to cross the Mersey was right below us. We ate under the light of chandeliers that night, with a stunning view across the river. The next morning, we met up for breakfast. Everybody had to be there, even though nobody wanted to be, and a number of players overslept. We were allowed to go back to bed afterwards but we had to get some food down us. That was why they wanted us at the hotel when we played late matches, to ensure ideal preparations for the long day ahead. Around noon a quiet walk was scheduled; we had to get outside for twenty minutes, get a little fresh air, do a little stretching, then lunch at half twelve. A lot of players returned to their rooms. The regular barber came to the hotel so that those who wanted to could get a haircut before the match. I sat down in his chair at the Radisson. Other times he would come to my house to cut my hair, as he did with several of the other players. Other people would come to the hotel as well. One guy brought the smartest pairs of shoes and set them out for us. Another guy had all the latest DVDs with him, a third arrived with diamonds in his suitcase, a jeweller selling watches and rings. A tailor would take our measurements and customise suits for us if we were interested. These were exclusive products, clearly. But everything was possible. Anything at all. No limits.

Three or four hours before the match we ate. Chicken and pasta. Always the same thing. Then back to the room to get ready. Shower and prepare properly. Then meet by the bus to drive through the city to the stadium.

I remember a packed Anfield singing 'You'll Never Walk Alone' with such force that the stadium was practically shaking as we sat in the dressing room. I almost felt bad for the Chelsea players. They were about to be crowned league champions but they had to be hearing it. There was an incredible roar from the fans when we came out on the pitch, before we lined up and the Champions League anthem was played. The community club against the billionaire's club. And I was ready.

We took the kick-off but Chelsea soon got a free-kick that Frank Lampard lifted into the area, yet Jerzy Dudek easily picked off the cross. And then I got the ball on my wing. It's only the third minute of play, and I felt this calmness. I saw things so clearly on the pitch, almost like in a silent film, just as I had done in the League Cup final earlier that year. So, when Lampard came towards me, I simply tapped the ball between his legs and collected it on the other side, like I had done to Erling

Ytterland at Nørvebana ten years earlier, and to Solskjær at the national-team training session. With my next touch I took the ball forward before centring to Steven Gerrard, who lifted the ball straight through to Milan Baroš with the outside of his boot. Milan Baroš was clean through on Čech. He managed to lift the ball over his countryman but was pulled down, and it would have been a penalty if Luis García hadn't managed to coax the ball barely over the goal line. We were uncertain but the referee, Ľuboš Micheľ, pointed to the centre circle. José Mourinho ran around shouting and protesting on the touchline. I like Mourinho, but I'm convinced that to this day he would claim the ball never crossed the line. 'The Ghost Goal', he dubbed it afterwards. But we were 1-0 up.

For the rest of the match Chelsea enjoyed the majority of possession, without being able to do much with it. I did four or five more nutmegs. I've always had a good eye for them. People don't expect that out of me because I'm not a polished technician, but it's something that's always come easy to me. And I love them. It's the ultimate humiliation. But to do it against Lampard and Chelsea in a semi-final of the Champions League … What can I say? It was a good year.

We needed to keep a clean sheet. When the fourth official signalled six minutes of added time, I was unmoved. They hammered in cross after cross, we blocked them out and cleared. We stood firm. The referee finally whistled for the end of the match. We were in the final of the Champions League.

The mood inside the dressing room was riotous. It hurt everywhere but the pain was numbed by the adrenaline. We bounced around and sang like we had done after the Juventus match. But this was even bigger, obviously. We had reached the final. Twenty-one years since the last time. If we won, we would be legends at the club. Much, much later, after the boots were off, the tape unwound, the socks and jerseys pulled off, and a long shower, we talked about the goal. We laughed at how furious Mourinho had been on the touchline. We took our time, we enjoyed it. It was the end of the season and when the adrenaline faded, I felt a tightness in my groin. Cramp pulsating through my calves. Toes aching. But we took a long time, like we usually did when we won. Then we enjoyed one another's company to the full. We got ready again. Deodorant and cologne. Shirts done up, one button at a time. We helped one another with the cufflinks, put on our smart trousers and knotted our ties, slipped into our shoes, felt the suit jacket hug the weary muscles. Everything was perfect.

We checked our hair in front of the mirror, then we went out to all the people still waiting for us. It was late evening, darkness had descended over the stadium, over the city, but we had all the time in the world.

Our opponent in the final was not decided until the following day. AC Milan had a 2–0 lead from the home leg, and most people must have thought the return leg in the Netherlands was going to be a formality. But PSV Eindhoven fought bravely. After 65 minutes they had clawed back Milan's lead. Now it was 2–2 on aggregate. But just when everyone seemed to be saving themselves for extra time, Massimo Ambrosini suddenly found himself free in front of the goal. One minute into stoppage time and Milan scored the goal they needed. The fact that Phillip Cocu struck back to make it 3-1 before the match concluded was of no consequence. Our opponent in Istanbul was going to be AC Milan. The Italians had won the Champions League trophy only two seasons earlier. Without a doubt they were huge favourites.

29

I WAS TWENTY YEARS OLD WHEN EINAR BAARDSEN ENTERED MY LIFE. He was a grown man of almost fifty. I was uneducated, had not even completed upper secondary school, and I may have been good at maths but I knew very little about financial matters. I didn't care either. I knew that I earned a lot money and that I was young. I was carefree and left someone else in charge of everything unrelated to sports, someone qualified to do that. That way I could concentrate fully and completely on football, which, after all, was the reason my financial situation was so good. I would have chosen to put the money in the bank or in some low-risk capital fund or something, and later invest it in property, but I knew that there were people who understood more about those things than I did, so I was more than willing to listen to them.

Baardsen was one of my closest friends, even though he was nearer my father's age. Year after year we stood side by side. I trusted him and gave him complete authority. I was happy to see him when I went to play internationals in Norway, happy for his monthly visits to Liverpool. I was proud to be represented by him, grateful for him being there to support me. He always praised me, said all the things I liked to hear. Every time we met up, there was a pile of documents to be dealt with. Money, large and small sums, had to be transferred here and there. If he arrived in Liverpool on the morning flight, he left the same night. If he arrived in the afternoon, he always spent the night at the Crowne Plaza down by Albert Dock and caught the early flight home the next morning. I wished we could have had more time together when he visited. We were mates, I suppose I must have looked up to him a little, but we rarely went out together or just chatted about stuff.

Baardsen knew that I wanted to have more distance from my mum when it came to business matters. He was well aware that he had initially been brought in because

Mum and Guri didn't get along very well; Baardsen's arrival was meant to spare me from getting caught in the middle. He began to exploit that division. When my mum told me she had not received the money she was due, he told me she was lying. He had paid her everything he was supposed to. He could produce emails and agreements which he believed could prove that he was telling the truth. The accusations against my family grew stronger and stronger. At one point he more or less said straight out that they were trying to pull the wool over my eyes, to exploit me.

One day Bengt Sæternes – a striker playing at Bodø/Glimt, but from Stavanger like Baardsen – contacted me to say that I had to be careful with this agent; that he had promised this, that, and the other, without the money ever turning up. Several people contacted me to say that there was something dodgy about the agent I had chosen. But Baardsen had no need to worry. I considered him a friend. And I've always been loyal to my friends. If anything, the warnings brought us closer together.

In retrospect, I've realised that he was entirely dependent on my money. Despite all the money he earned off me, he had massive financial difficulties. And thanks to my money he was able to stay afloat for as long as he did. In February 2005 he had his agent licence suspended for one year by the Football Association of Norway. It concerned matters I thought were incredibly dull, like insufficient insurance cover, use of invalid representation contracts, and failure to duly submit representation contracts. When he explained to me that it was merely a matter of formalities, I believed him. I was not a great fan of the NFF in any case. If I was left to choose between them and my friend, I knew whose side I would be on.

30

ARIANA WAS THE FIRST THING I HAD TATTOOED ON ME. OCTOBER 2004. Until then my body had been equally pale all over, but I visited a tattoo artist in Liverpool and asked him to ink the name of my daughter on my right forearm. It had been two months without her. I watched as the man with latex gloves traced the letters of her name around my arm. I couldn't be with her as much time as I wanted but this way she would be with me everywhere I went. I remember scoring against Blackburn that weekend and raising my arm in the air: Ariana.

I hadn't actually planned to get any more back then. At least not as many as I've got now. It just snowballed. The biggest one is inked across my chest: *Believe in yourself*. Every time I go to have a shower, I see it in the mirror. And it reminds me of who I am. Of what I've been through, not least during my childhood, and what I've achieved despite all that.

I like statement tattoos. People might think they're daft but I don't care; it's my body. To me they're not just empty phrases, they're words that carry meaning. *Without struggle there is no progress. Everything happens for a reason. Giving up was never an option.* That last one is tattooed down the right side of my chest. *Brothers for life.* Both my brother and I have that at the back of our upper arms. I got a tattoo of Louise Angelica's name shortly after we met in 2012 and people thought it was a bad idea. *What if you change your mind? What if you split up?* But I don't think like that. No matter what happens, she's been an important part of my life. She arrived in my life and showed me that the opportunity for happiness was still there. She gave me my self-confidence back. She changed my life. Even if we split up one day, God forbid, she did that for me. She would still mean all of that to me. That's why I tattooed her name along my rib, to make sure it really hurt. I had *Louise* tattooed in Lillestrøm but God, did it hurt. I had to stop after *Louise* and for a while I considered leaving off *Angelica*. Louise is what I call her, after all. But that would have been spineless of me. She's the woman I love. We live together. So finally I had the tattoo completed in Oslo: *Louise Angelica*.

I have our birthdays tattooed in Greek characters on either side of my neck. And I have *You'll Never Walk Alone* tattooed down my left leg. On my left arm I have the names and birthdates of my two youngest children, Emma and Patrick, who I don't live with either.

I carry around a lot of guilt about my children. I had one daughter in Ålesund and two children in London. That's the way my life turned out. I have three children and I don't get to see any of them grow up. I did abandon them, in a way. I divorced their mothers and I've lived in different countries than them. I can't walk in now and interfere in their upbringing, I have no right to do that. I get that. The opportunity has passed me by. I don't get to see them sitting in the kitchen doing their homework. I'm not part of their everyday conversations. I'm not there when they have to go back to school after the summer holidays, nervous to be starting a new year. The two youngest still live in London, so I talk to them mostly on FaceTime and Skype. Every time we're about to wrap up, I tell them I love them. I don't want them to wonder, like I did with my dad. I say it every single time: *I love you. I miss you.*

No, I have to stop there. I'm not telling things the way they really are. I'm more like my dad than I care to admit. Yes, I tell my children I love them, but it's through a screen. Face to face, I find it incredibly difficult. I love them and I'd do anything for them, obviously. Still it's almost impossible for me to say those three words when I'm standing right in front of them. The same goes for physical intimacy. I want nothing more than to wrap my arms around my teenage daughter when she's having a tough time but I can't bring myself to do it. I'm ashamed of that and I'm trying to work on it in order to be a better dad. I don't know why I think it's so difficult to express my feelings in that way, but it's the same with my sisters, who are so important to me. 'Hug your sister, Jonnen,' Mum says. 'Come on now!'

But I can't do it.

I know that the children are good where they are. That's the most important thing. But I miss them.

The lid on the black box has started to come loose. Memories slip out. Working on this book has meant that I've had to dig up things I would have preferred to forget. But I have to try to understand why things have turned out the way they did.

Why did I make the choices I did? And recently, I think a lot about children. I think a lot about my dad. I get sudden flashes of being bullied at school. Dark memories come to the surface. Standing in an empty corridor at school, someone has stolen my gym bag. During the lunch break I wait to be picked for the football match, but they just ignore me. I wait for the school bus, but when the doors open, the other children don't let me on. They shout that I'm not getting on with them – they laugh, 'Shut the door!' – and for some reason the bus driver doesn't intervene, just as the teachers at school don't. Instead I have to run along the side of the road, trailing after the bus.

I have no choice. I can no longer block it all out.

31

THE LIVERPOOL FIRE BRIGADE SHOWERED THE AIR WITH WATER before our plane took off from John Lennon Airport. A guard of honour, with fire trucks on either side, spraying a magnificent arch of water over us. Four hours later we arrived at Istanbul Atatürk airport. We were met by a bus on the landing strip, then driven straight to the hotel with a police escort. With the exception of the fire brigade, this was normal procedure when we played Champions League matches abroad. I can't count how many cities and countries I've been to where I've seen everything through a window at top speed. Security guards and cameras. At the hotel, we were shielded from the other guests. For the most part, we remained behind closed doors in our rooms. We had two floors at our disposal and meals were also served there. We lived in our own bubble. If we had to take the lift down to the dining hall, we would run into people in the lift, and the idea was that the tiniest thing that could disturb our calm had to be weeded out. We had separate rooms but got up early to have breakfast together like before all evening matches, not because we wanted to, but just to get something to eat. With food in our bellies, we returned to our rooms and went back to sleep. The pre-match preparations had to be the same as all the evening matches: a couple of hours later we went for a walk in a well-planned, closed-off, secure area around the back of the hotel. Just to loosen up, no more than fifteen to twenty minutes. Benítez was there, approaching individual players, putting his arm around them, myself included, very relaxed: 'How do you feel? Are you ready?' He knew that this was the biggest match of my career and he wanted to show his faith in me. I knew I was going to start the match. I felt good.

Afterwards there was stretching, then a quick team meeting at the hotel to discuss our opponents. Benítez wanted speed on the wings, he told us, so he was going to play a 4-4-1-1 formation. Harry Kewell and I were going to play on the left.

It was a surprising formation, only two in the middle against AC Milan's diamond. He wanted speed on the outside and Luis García to form the creative link between the midfield and Milan Baroš in attack. That meant some highly unexpected news, Didi Hamann was left on the bench. Didi was one of my best friends on the team. I looked over at him but he didn't bat an eyelid.

Then back to the room for more rest, three or four hours. As usual we were called together for the final meal before the match about four hours before kick-off. Chicken and pasta. Then back to our rooms. I listened to music, like I always did. Nothing I like too much or that gets me too geared up, but a playlist that someone has put together with whatever's on the radio at the time. At this point I always start to sense the anticipation, but I have to restrain my excitement. I don't want to wear myself out. Before every match I do the same. All right, so it was the biggest football match of my life but I had to do the same thing I always did. No routines could be broken. So I took a long shower. Not too hot, because then I would get a little tired. I stretched carefully in the shower. As usual I also spent a good deal of time after the shower getting ready. Gel and wax in my hair. A little cologne. Deodorant. When I came out on the pitch, I had to be in mint condition, impeccable. Always. People think it's vanity that makes us smarten up for matches but it's not like that, at least that's not the only reason. Preparation is a kind of safeguard. Nothing was to be left to chance.

When I set foot on the pitch, met by the roar of some 70,000 mad fans, I had to be armed, down to the last detail. I had to keep my head cool and clear. I don't think people quite realise how ferocious these matches could be. I was also known to be a tough, physical player; I couldn't let myself do anything haphazardly. I had to be armed. My body was going to be pushed till it could hardly take any more. Two matches a week, often. Every time the body was stretched to breaking point. The muscles screamed in pain. The back ached. It was a matter of being smart on the pitch, though you never knew what your opponent might do. Calves slamming into each other, grown men launching themselves into tackles, sliding along the grass at top speed with all their weight behind them, hitting an ankle, a knee, a thigh. You could go up for a header and he might come charging up behind you, two skulls colliding with a hollow thud. I've heard the sounds of every injury. I've seen a foot broken right off, a limp football boot hanging from the calf. Anything can happen. In every match, anything can happen.

Before we left the hotel, there was another meeting. The team selection was announced. Benítez went through tactics and what to do in dead-ball situations. From there we went straight on the bus. Tracksuits with the Champions League logo on them had been specially made for the occasion. Very little was said on the bus. I looked out of the window and saw large groups of fans trying to get to the stadium on foot. It was chaos, they were walking in the middle of the road. Through the glass I could hear them singing. The tension really began to build.

Once we reach the stadium, I have to be first off the bus. It's been like that for as long as I can remember. I have to be the first one off or it means bad luck.

In the dressing room I found my boots polished and waiting for me. I had asked Nike to stitch Ariana into the leather, along with the Norwegian flag. We got changed without much chatter. Someone clipped their nails, like they did before every match. Others checked their laces or just sat listening to music on their headphones. A few placed religious symbols near their spot, some prayed, others had family pictures they put up. I didn't have anything special with me but I did have my ritual: left sock first, then the right. Then left boot before the right one. For three and a half years I had been doing the same thing so my preparations were automatic now, but I'd sense it if I ever messed up the order and then I'd have to start from scratch. I'd have to take off my boots and socks until I was sitting in my bare feet then start over. Everything had to be absolutely perfect. The left boot had to be a little tighter than the right.

We ran out to do our warm-up. The stadium was nearly full already and the intensity was insane, but there had been reports of people having problems getting to the match. We ran over and applauded our travelling supporters. After that I don't remember much because by then I had disappeared into my own bubble. One of the coaches led the warm-up, which as usual lasted around twenty minutes. Back in the dressing room, someone was getting a massage; I remember smelling the oil. Others stretched or double-checked their laces. All I did was lace my boots again until they were tight enough, put on my shin guards. And waited. Always waiting, it takes too long for my liking. Steven Gerrard got up and wished us luck: 'This is the biggest game of our lives. Come on!' A whistling sound in the dressing room announced that it was time to queue up in the tunnel, which meant there were no more than a few minutes until the start of the match. I got as close to the front as possible in the row of players. As always I wanted to get on to the pitch quickly. In Istanbul I was third in the queue, behind Gerrard and Jerzy Dudek. Then came Milan. Big names. Andrea Pirlo, Paolo Maldini, Andriy Shevchenko, Clarence Seedorf, Hernán Crespo, Kaká, Cafu. Now we were playing for the same trophy. It was displayed at the opening of the tunnel ahead of us. I heard the Champions League anthem being played in the stadium and the hairs on my arms stood on end. I felt so good. We went out. You were not meant to touch the trophy as you walked past, everyone knew that. I guess it means bad luck. I didn't see it because I was right at the front but Gennaro Gattuso, Milan's midfield terrier, was unable to restrain himself. He touched the cup as he passed on the way out on the pitch.

The cameras flashing in the dark. The TV cameras following us out. The sea of people. I was ready.

We started with the ball but Kaká quickly got hold of it on my wing, and I ran in hot pursuit. Djimi Traoré arrived and brought him down. Not even half a minute had lapsed. Pirlo put the ball down and struck the free-kick firmly into the area. At the same time Maldini made a run and nobody picked him up so he was able to create a bit of space for himself. Xabi Alonso and I raced over but he struck the volley with his right foot before we could reach him. I saw the ball go in the far corner. It was 1–0. Fifty-two seconds had passed of what was supposed to be the most important match of our lives. The Italian team had already shown themselves to be tactically superior and exploited the fact that we relied on zonal marking. After the restart things didn't get much better. Gerrard and Xabi Alonso fought like tigers but were outnumbered in the midfield by Pirlo, Seedorf and a sublime Kaká. They didn't have much of a chance. I heard Gerrard and Carragher shouting at Luis García to help defend the middle and we picked up a little. Gerrard knocked in a corner from the right that I struck perfectly from twenty yards, but my volley was blocked. Later Luis García received a pass and was close to pulling away from Alessandro Nesta inside the eighteen-yard box. As Nesta went down on the moist grass, the ball appeared to strike his right elbow and García shouted loudly for a penalty, but there was no reaction from the referee. Instead, Milan surged into attack – mere seconds had passed after our fairly justified penalty shout, when Crespo, on loan from Chelsea, made it 2–0. Five minutes later he added another to make it 3–0 after a lovely through-pass from Kaká that Carragher couldn't quite reach. Crespo's chip over Dudek was sublime. There was one minute left before the break.

At 1–0, I thought there was plenty of time to do something. At 2–0, I was concerned. When they scored their third goal, I had no doubt. This game was over.

I wanted to get away more than anything. I didn't want to be caught on camera, be seen on the TV screens. 'I ran around the pitch but any kind of system had long since disappeared. I was not looking forward to hearing Benítez tell us off in the interval. Like most of the players, I was worried about being substituted. Because clearly something had to be done. When the half-time whistle sounded I thought: *Now what? God, we're up against the best defensive team in Europe. And we're down by three goals.*

On the way to the dressing room I heard Gattuso shouting. I didn't understand Italian at that point but it's obvious that he's celebrating: *We've won this!*

32

I WANT TO TALK ABOUT MY MUM. A LOT OF PEOPLE HAVE AN OPINION about my mum, particularly in Norway. I realise that. She was the one who took care of me and my brother. People react when they hear how hard she pushed me, for example how she stood at the top of the hill near our house timing me, shouting and urging me on, from a very young age. In her eyes she's also the one who forced me onto the plane and made me leave my friends in Ålesund to play for Monaco. And I never heard the end of it. I was a mummy's boy. I was tied to her apron strings. I dyed my hair whenever she did. Stuff like that. I get why people said those things but for a long time it was the two of us against the world.

When I went to Liverpool, I asked her to take a step back from my career. I asked her to just be my mum. It wasn't the first time I asked her. Or the last.

I love her but we have a complicated relationship. She's really stubborn and sometimes she doesn't know what to do with all that stubbornness. She still can't stay out of things. She wants to be involved in everything, including who she thinks I should be with. Often she'll take little pokes at me. She'll tell me she deserves the full credit for my success. She says she regrets making me get on the plane all those years ago because all the attention that came from of it has destroyed so many things in our family. And it's true that all the scandal has hurt those closest to me, like my sisters, who are eight and twelve years younger than me. My youngest sister was bullied from the time she started school. They would shout at her and push her around, say our family was filth, that she didn't deserve to live, that they would kill us. For a while she had regular appointments with the head teacher every Monday to discuss what the papers had written about us over the weekend, so that she could get to grips with it. If she came to school wearing a new jacket, they'd shout at her that everything she got was because of her brother. It's horrible to think about.

I wouldn't have mentioned it if they hadn't gone public and talked about their experiences. My oldest sister had to get picked up by mum from a graduation event because she had been surrounded by a big mob of students pouring beer over her and shouting nasty things about our family. It got so bad that they had to move away from Ålesund … I can't stand to think about it. I want to say sorry, even though it's not my fault.

But when my Mum and I have a row, we say things we don't mean. She implies that at the end of the day, those events were my fault. That really hurts. I feel that I've contributed a lot to my family, including financially. And she hasn't exactly been a shrinking violet over the years, either. For example, she published an autobiography called 'Just a mum'. That's her right but I haven't read it.

At the same time, I've responded by saying things in in the heat of battle. *Ungrateful old bag! Now I know why Dad left you!* That last one is probably the worst, but sometimes I just can't take it. Mum is so publicity-seeking and attention-grabbing that in a lot of cases I would say that's the reason things have turned out the way they did.

But obviously I can see that we're more alike than I'd care to admit. I'm stubborn, I love the attention. We're both strong. Neither of us are good at keeping our mouths shut. And I have no doubt that she has had to put up with a lot, as a woman in a male-dominated industry.

And I want her to be my mum. I love her very much.

33

IT'S THE SECOND HALF. NINE MINUTES HAVE ELAPSED. I HAVE possession on the left. I try to knock the ball in, but the cross is blocked off by Cafu and it ends up bouncing back to me again. This time the ball sails into the area. Gerrard rises into the air. He meets the ball perfectly with his head. It travels in an elegant curve into the Milan keeper Dida's left corner. Gerrard has scored. We've cut their lead. Gerrard waves his arms in the air to fire up the crowd while he and the rest of the team run back to our half. We want to get the match restarted as quickly as possible. We're full of energy. But we look at the Milan players, and soon realise they can live with it. Give them their one goal, they think. Yet the tempo in their passing slows. They don't run as much as they did in the first half.

Two minutes later Vladimír Šmicer launches a long-range shot. Dida can't stop it. It's 3–2. It's bloody well 3–2! And now we notice the Milan players getting stressed. They're yelling and shouting at each other. Gattuso in particular. Not that it helps. Only minutes later he is desparately tugging Gerrard back as our captain bursts through the middle of their penalty area. The referee points to the penalty spot.

Xabi Alonso is to take it. His first penalty in professional football. In the final of the Champions League. Just look at the images on TV, check out how nervous the poor lad is. The drama is almost unbearable. If he converts the spot-kick, we'll have cancelled out Milan's 3–0 lead. I smell the grass, smoke from the terraces. The Italian supporters are whistling and trying to put him off. None of us look at each other, afraid of bringing bad luck or afraid of revealing the dread we feel. I see Xabi Alonso step back from the ball on the penalty spot. Dida looks huge in the goal. I can hardly breathe. He runs towards the ball, shoots it hard to the right of the Brazilian keeper but Dida reaches down, stops the shot. In that moment, it feels like my heart is about to stop. But before I have time to think, Xabi races for the rebound as though his life depends on it, and he reaches the ball with his left foot. Getting it over Dida is a massive task, as his 6ft 5in frame charges for the loose ball. Xabi hammers the ball up and into the netting. Boom! Unbelievable. We've cancelled out their lead. It's 3–3. In six magical minutes we've clawed our way back against Milan. And there's still loads of time left. But we're exhausted. We have to collect ourselves. Playing catch-up has cost us. We feel it now. We're at rock-bottom. We play on instinct. Gerrard drops to right-back to stop Milan substitute Serginho and he launches himself into the tackle every time the powerful Brazilian comes down the wing like a freight train. Carragher plays with his socks rolled down, a symbol of our battle to the bone. It's blood, sweat and tears. I get a chance to shoot. I hammer it with my left foot from twenty-something yards but Dida just manages to get his hands up in time to stop the projectile. It could have decided everything. With ten minutes remaining in normal time, cramp begins to set in. First in the calves, then the back of one thigh, then the groin. But I don't ask to be substituted. There's no chance of that happening. I'd have to break a leg before signalling to be taken off.

Not much happens in extra time. It's as though everything has been spent in this insane match. Both sides are somehow content. Then Milan get a glorious chance. Andriy Shevchenko heads a cross from Serginho and Jerzy Dudek makes a miraculous save. Not content with that, he also stops the rebound that Shevchenko fires from half a yard in front of the goal line. Later Dudek told us that he just shut his eyes and stretched his arms to the right.

The referee whistles the end of extra time. And I immediately know what to do. I want to take one of the penalties.

We gather by the substitutes' bench. I see Benítez wandering around with his notepad. I follow him with my gaze. Then he looks up at me. I nod at him. And he writes down my name as our third penalty taker. I'm so proud. For me, it's an honour to be trusted in a situation like that. I'm not afraid of missing. The thought doesn't enter my mind. But one thing worries me as I get treatment from the physiotherapist: cramp.

We line up on the halfway line, side by side with our arms around one another. I'm standing between Vladimír Šmicer and Xabi Alonso. Dida tries to get the referee to let him touch the ball but he has to relent, and the two keepers exchange a few words before Dudek takes his place in goal. Milan are up first. Serginho is to take it.

He walks slowly across the pitch. Only our fans can be heard. They are singing so loudly that the noise billows across the pitch. As soon as he reaches the ball, which the referee has placed on the penalty spot, Dudek runs up to touch it but the referee directs him to take his place on the goal line. Dudek takes his time getting into position. The crowd whistle. I don't know if it's the Liverpool fans trying to psyche out Serginho or the Milan fans upset at our keeper. Serginho spends a long time getting the ball to sit the way he wants it to on the penalty spot. Finally he takes one last look at it and turns to take his run-up. Dudek is waving his arms around like a windmill. Serginho lines up, puts his hands on his hips and sees Dudek waving his arms even more and bouncing erratically along the goal line. Serginho runs up, side-foots it, but the ball disappears high above the right corner of the goal, sending him into a state of despair.

Dietmar Hamann scores on our first penalty, even though Dida gets a hand to it. One-nil to us. Then it's Andrea Pirlo's turn. Dudek picks up the ball and hands it to him before walking back to the goal. The whistling from the stands is deafening. I realise now that it's our fans. They're the ones who make themselves heard; they're doing everything in their power to help us. Dudek clowns around on the goal line, bounces back and forth, still waving his arms, and I don't know if that's what does the trick, but Pirlo hits a rather weak penalty that he gets a glove to and saves. I see Pirlo take a deep sigh as he walks away. Djibril Cissé is our next taker. He's asked by the referee to reposition the ball on the penalty spot. I worry it will put him off, but he places the ball safely in Dida's left corner, seemingly unmoved by the circumstances. Dida goes one way, the ball the other. We're ahead 2–0 on penalties. Jon Dahl Tomasson converts his for Milan. 2–1. Then it's my turn.

It's a long way from the halfway line to the penalty spot when you have to take a penalty in the final of the Champions League. I try to act as though I've got everything under control, but I don't know exactly where to look. Step by step I move towards the penalty area. Dida collects the ball behind the goal and throws it out towards the penalty spot. If I score, it could prove to be the decisive penalty. We would win if they failed to score their next attempt. Then I would have decided the final. I try not to think about it. I just walk. Thirty seconds it takes me to get all the way there. I still haven't decided how I'm going to take the penalty. Normally I would always go for power. But now I'm a little concerned that my leg won't support me. Would cramp kick in if I hit it with all I've got? During the long, dreaded walk from the halfway line to collect the ball I bgin to think. I could do a Panenka. It's a penalty where you just chip the ball softly up the middle of the goal, named after Antonín Panenka who, with ice in his veins, scored the decisive penalty in that manner when Czechoslovakia beat West Germany in the final of the European Championship in 1976. It will never work if Dida doesn't move, I think. He's tall and could make use of his reach. He could throw his body back. I place the ball on the penalty spot. Still haven't decided. Madness. I'm afraid to do what I normally do, just hammer the ball into the goal.

But a Panenka... I'd be remembered for that. I place the ball, then put the thought out of my head. I have to take the safer option, for the team. I glance at the referee to see if he's happy with the placement of the ball then take a few steps back. Only when I turn towards Dida do I decide. I'm just going to place the ball. Locate it low into his right corner. I take a few stuttering steps then race towards the ball. I side-foot it. It's not a bad penalty. It's low and away from him but Dida gets there. I see him get a hand on it. And then I feel my world unravelling. I wish the crowd would just swallow me up as I stare into the darkness. I don't hear a thing. I try to get some air into my lungs. The expressions of my teammates on the halfway line are unmistakable. Despair. I understand them. I should just have hammered the bloody ball into the net. I shuffle back towards the halfway line. Kaká passes me on the way to take his penalty, but I don't look at him. There is less pressure on him now. Because of me. The vice we had them in has loosened. The entire decisive penalty shootout is in danger of turning. Gerrard comes over and pats me on the head but it doesn't help. Carragher a little less diplomatically asks me why I went right. 'Didn't you see that he went right on Xabi's penalty, and on Didi's and Cissé's?' I didn't reply. Instead I thought: *Why the hell didn't you tell me that before I took the penalty? It's a little late now! But I should have seen it.* As always, Carra was right.

Kaká converted his penalty even with Dudek moving like a jellyfish on the line before he struck it. We had been so close to deciding the match, I had been. Instead it was suddenly 2–2 on penalties now. Milan's manager, Carlo Ancelotti, is moving restlessly in front of the bench, now with his back to us. It was Šmicer's turn. The pressure on him was immense. The club had signalled that they weren't going to need his services going forward. In the final home league match he had not been selected for the team. Vladi had been furious with Benítez, but the only thing that mattered now was getting the ball in the net. Again Dida dove to the right but Šmicer placed the ball safely in the opposite corner. Which meant that Shevchenko had to net his to keep Milan from losing. Milan Baroš and I couldn't do anything but hold each other as Shevchenko crossed the pitch. He ran his hand through his hair, adjusted his jersey. I have no doubt that the improbable save by Dudek half a minute before the referee whistled the end of extra time was in the back of his mind. He looked over at the referee, then set off. His penalty was terrible. Weak and down the middle but not in a high arch like with a Panenka, it stayed low. Dudek stopped it rather easily. We rushed towards him and my miss was forgotten. We screamed in joy, roaring and practically butting heads to find an outlet for all the tension that had suddenly been released. We celebrated on the athletics track in front of our fans. I was crying. I looked up at them and saw that they were crying too. They shook their heads in disbelief at what they had witnessed. I've seen the images on TV. We screamed and ran round like idiots. I wanted to be drowned in the red sea of happiness in the stands. I wanted to be up there with them. I could see their faces, shining with joy. Everything swaying and rocking. The memory is still hazy, the details dispersed in happiness and exhaustion. We were presented with our gold medals. We stood on a podium. I was wearing something ridiculous on my head, supporters' gear, a cheap replica of a hat from the Ottoman Empire or something. I must have got it from one of our fans in the stands, or from Luis García, I can't sift through the details. We bounced around and danced on the podium. Finally the burly, Swedish president of UEFA, Lennart Johansson, handed the cup to Stevie. When he lifted it above his head, everything exploded. There was a gigantic boom and red confetti rained down from everywhere, red and white smoke shot up into the night sky of Istanbul, before drifting back down and settling over us. We had been part of a miracle. We were the kings of Europe. Stevie kissed the cup. I stood next to him. I remember the feel of the silver handles, the weight of the cup when he passed it to me. I could see my face mirrored back at me when I went to kiss it, and for first time I liked my reflection. Then I got to raise the cup to the heavens, as if to show everyone: Look here, God or whoever else is up there, this is ours!

We would celebrate, some of us for weeks. The following day we would arrive in Liverpool and board the bus amidst a staggering crowd of people. Hands reaching out to touch the bus, making it rock side to side, but we just enjoyed it. An estimated 1.2 million people lined the streets. I remember Stevie saying that the celebration reminded him of the pictures of the Beatles he had seen on TV as a child. I looked across the sea of people and felt loved by everyone. We would dance on tables into the wee hours of the night, meet famous actors and performers who joined the celebration when we returned to Liverpool, that was how it would be. But on this night in Istanbul, we barely managed to make it to the dressing room. It looked like a battlefield. Most of us had cuts that had to be seen to, there were scrapes, ice, bandages, sweat, dirt and a lot of tears.

At the hotel, food and drink was enticingly set out for our celebration. But the mere sight of it made me tired, so tired. I had no energy left. My body felt like a rag. My head was frazzled. I went up to my room. It was the middle of the night. The metropolis of Istanbul was shining all the way to the horizon. Life outside was pulsating. I sat on the bed in the dark. I don't get a chance to remember what I was thinking. My head was filled with deafening silence. And then I slept.

34

EVER SINCE I WAS LITTLE, I HAD DREAMED OF THE DAY I COULD BUY A Ferrari. The name itself had a power of attraction over me. Ferrari had a ring of speed and excitement about it. And the logo! The prancing black stallion on a yellow background, shaped like a coat-of-arms, with the Italian colours at the top. In a way, the logo in itself contained everything I could have dreamed of.

Playing at Liverpool provided me with a salary that was more than generous. Having a wealthy lifestyle was something I had no problem adjusting to. I didn't struggle with it. I was obsessed with clothes and watches. There was one downside: the need to give life a kind of distance, due to the vulnerability you could feel at times. Having a well-tailored suit, a haircut or a shave if you're nervous or uneasy, that actually helps. Personally, it was also because there were plenty of days when I couldn't stand to see my own face in the mirror in the morning. Often the only thing I saw was the pale, ginger boy from the schoolyard. Now I had the opportunity to buy myself some self-confidence. Like the other players, I shopped at the Cricket fashion store in the Cavern Quarter, an exclusive shop that sold clothes and accessories by high-end designers like Saint Laurent, DSquared2, Balenciaga and Armani. They would open the store for us after closing time so that we could shop in peace. I started to buy watches: Rolex, Jacob & Co, brands like that. Wristwatches you wore as jewellery. The watches were often purchased from the jewellers who came to the hotel before matches, or they came to our homes. That's the way it worked. No matter what you wanted to do or buy, the club or a teammate always had a contact who could sort out what you wanted. Everything was catered for. We didn't have to think of the trivialities. It was lovely, but obviously those sorts of things didn't exactly lessen the sense of living in an egocentric bubble. To this day when I fly to Liverpool, a customs officer will come and lead me past the queue at passport control. And I have to admit: I kind of like it.

I even had my own taxi driver, Bernie, who drove my family and friends everywhere, who picked me up on nights out. He was a brilliant guy, chubby and cheerful and extremely loyal. He was always there for my nearest and dearest.

After our success in the Champions League I was not exactly earning less. For each match we won in the Champions League, we received a bonus. For winning the whole thing – the first Liverpool team to do so for 21 years – we each received a bonus of around £150,000.

Designer clothes and watches were one thing, but for me the ultimate sign of success was a Ferrari. I thought that nobody who saw me in a Ferrari would remember the boy who used to hide in a hoody. And for those sitting around at Miller's in Ålesund, the ones who had shouted that I shouldn't play for Liverpool, if my success in itself wasn't enough for them, I would have the car that erased every doubt: I was a champion.

My voice was shaking when I rang the dealer. I had decided on the F430 model. And it had to be red. There was no other option. A white Ferrari? You don't buy a Ferrari in order to blend in with the surroundings. It had to be seen. And heard. I remember when I turned the key for first time, the roar of the engine under the bonnet. A V8 with 500 horsepower. The feeling is indescribable. The smell of the leather seats, which enveloped your body when you sat on them, the steering wheel that made you feel like a racing driver.

The guy at the dealership could arrange to have an F430 model sent from Germany. It cost £150,000. It was the best money I'd spent in my entire life. I was like a little kid when someone finally rang to say that the lorry was on its way. I was jumping with joy. I went out in the front garden to watch for it, listening for the sound of the lorry. It was sunny that day, I remember. Oh, the feeling of a red Ferrari backing down the loading ramp onto the drive outside your house.

In the first few days, practically the only thing I did in my spare time was cruise around in it. Stomp on the accelerator when the lights turned green, feel the acceleration. Drive up and down the streets. Show off to my friends and whoever else wanted to see it. I had won the Champions League. Look! Look how beautiful it is!

The following week I was off to Norway, first to play a World Cup qualifier against

Italy at Ullevaal. I was looking forward to the match. I loved national-team gatherings, I always have. But I'd barely had the car for a week. After the game I was staying in Norway on holiday. Was I supposed to go the entire summer without my amazing, beautiful car? It was brand new. No, that would not do. I was staying at the Plaza Hotel in Oslo, so I had the car delivered there. A company picked up the Ferrari at my home in Liverpool, loaded it onto a lorry, transported it across the North Sea by boat and then on to the hotel. It cost a fair bit, I have to admit. And there's no point denying that with an income like mine, an extravagant lifestyle went with it. But I could afford it. And now I had my car. I told the parking attendants at the hotel that they could take it for a spin if they promised to keep a close eye on the marvel of a car. Every day they handed over the Ferrari, clean and shiny. I was a happy man.

Pretty soon the newspapers started to write about it. I had no problem with that. I had driven the car to be seen. Obviously. I had no intention of keeping a low profile. I was single and out to impress. Why shouldn't I be able to do that? How was I to know that the journalists were going to make such a fuss about it. If they could afford it, most of them would buy one too, wouldn't they? And all my teammates at Liverpool had similar cars, some had several. Steven Gerrard, for example – a man nobody would call flashy – had a Porsche, a Bentley, an Aston Martin convertible, a Mercedes and a Land Rover. So I didn't give it much thought.

I got a parking ticket and the papers wrote about it. The manager of the bank I had parked outside of received a little free publicity when he told the journalist that he would pay the fine. Later they wrote that I got a ticket outside a a restaurant called Mucho Mas where I'd been for dinner with my friend, the singer Sandra Lyng Haugen. For a while it was as though the journalists had started a newspaper devoted to parking. The car was reported being seen everywhere, but often it wasn't me driving, but some of the employees at the hotel. It wasn't as though I was the only one in Oslo with an expensive car, but obviously I was the one they were interested in. As I said, it was fine by me. I was the one that bought the fancy car. I hadn't envisaged that there would be stories about me being the biggest idiot in the world because I had spent my Champions League bonus on a boyhood dream instead of investing in property or something more sensible, more mature and something offering tax advantages. I'd rather have fun.

35

TWO DAYS BEFORE WE WERE DUE TO TRAVEL TO ISTANBUL TO PLAY the final of the Champions League, I received a text from Einar Baardsen. He kept it brief; there were some papers I had to sign. I thought it could wait. I was about to play the most important match of my career. I could just deal with the documents later. Truth be told, I found it a little strange that my agent was disturbing me with a matter like that at a moment like that. Following the training session the next day, I received another text message. And when I arrived in Istanbul there were even more. It must be urgent, I realised. But good God, I was at the hotel, preparing to play in the final of the world's biggest club tournament. I didn't reply. On the very morning of the match, the phone rang. I was in my room. It was Baardsen. He was pretty upset. Let's just say that he told me off. He was clearly in a predicament. Around £8,000 needed to be transferred, he told me. He needed my signature and he needed it at once. I was a little confused by his tone but I just wanted the matter settled. I was going to play a match against AC Milan in front of a packed stadium. An entire world was going to be watching. Cafu was going to be storming down my wing, and it might open up space for me to attack.

'What do I need to do?' I said. He told me to go down to reception and he'd fax over some papers. I had to sign them, then ask the hotel staff to either fax them back or have them scanned and emailed to him.

'And I need to do this now?'

'Yes, right now.'

'But we're supposed to stay on the two floors they've reserved for us,' I tried to explain. There were no two ways about it. I'd just have to find my way down to reception. Once there, I was given the papers, stood at the counter and signed both sides like I'd been told.

After that incident, I started having doubts' as to whether Einar Baardsen was really my friend. But every time I questioned him about something, he came back with a believable answer. He was willing to do whatever it took. I realised that in retrospect. And this was the man in charge of every contract, every agreement and every investment of mine, from the time I was twenty. I'd stood by him loyally. I was a damned idiot. That's what I was.

After the week of celebrations, after all the commotion from the victory had settled down, I meticulously went through everything that had happened between Baardsen and me and realised that there had never been any friendship. Slowly the pieces of the puzzle fell into place. That was why the restaurant visits were so few, why his trips were so brief. I grew more and more upset as the situation became clear. He had been using me the entire time. I had no choice. I sent a text message to Baardsen to say that I wanted to end our partnership: *I've figured out what you've been up to.* I hired lawyers to take care of the matter. Their task was to go through my contracts, creditors and accounts. It turned out to be a practically impenetrable forest, with Baardsen's finances completely fused with mine, except that almost exclusively I was the one supplying the money. I remember arriving at their law office in Oslo. I was going to find out the results of their investigation. I was anxious but in a good mood. Because even though the money had vanished, I did earn over twenty million kroner (nearly £2million at the time, over £2.5million today) a year before tax, so it couldn't be all that bad.

'Take a seat,' they said. There were four or five of them in the room. One of them, I can't remember who, took the floor. He said that this wasn't pleasant for him but I had seemingly accrued a debt of thirty-five million kroner (over £3million). I heard him announce the figures. Then I started to cry. I sat there in their law office and cried. In order to repay the debt, I'd have to earn seventy million kroner gross, I calculated. I was surrounded by men in suits. I'd been a pro footballer for six seasons, five of them at Liverpool. I had just won the Champions League, and what I was left with was a debt of over £3million.

When I stopped crying, I pounded my fist on the table as hard as I could. The coffee cups clattered on the saucers. 'Okay,' I said. 'I'm still young. I make good money. Set up a payment plan, then I'll play some football and pay off this fucking debt.'

I could live with losing the money. I could even live with being cheated. But my embarrassment at being so gullible was hard to swallow. Now everyone's thoughts were confirmed: *That Riise guy, not very bright, is he? Squandered away all his money.* People stopped me in the streets: *Should I send you some money?* And I get it. They didn't mean any harm, it was a joke, but I was so ashamed that I just wanted to vanish. I wanted to cease to exist. I wanted to leave, go somewhere where nobody knew who I was. Where there were no papers, no radio, TV or internet. Because it was everywhere, my stupidity. And Einar Baardsen was to blame. I thought Baardsen had genuinely liked me. I thought he had cared. Maybe that was why I never took a closer look at things. I wanted him to be my friend. I didn't want to know, and when I finally faced up to reality, it all became public knowledge. And it almost became too much for me. It was unbearable. There was no way out. No light at the end of the tunnel.

Why didn't I do a runner? I had a daughter. I had to play football, I had responsibilities. I couldn't run away from everything.

I took him to court and he was acquitted: the statute of limitations had expired, I had signed everything without proper scrutiny, and anyway, the money was gone. The damage had been done. The result of the lawsuit was not that important to me. But he tormented my thoughts. He had set out to ruin me, my family and my future. My future investments no longer existed. Equally as bad, he had tried to sow discord between me and my family and he had tried to destroy my reputation. I wanted to ruin his life like he had tried to ruin mine.

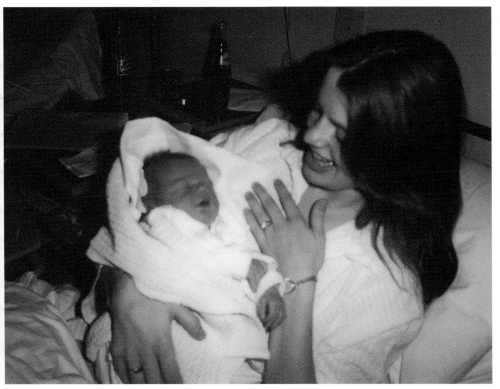

Blissful baby and toddler years in Norway with mum and dad. Childhood and adolescence
would pose more challenges.

Same stadium, different teams. Playing for Monaco against Nancy, then scoring for Liverpool in Monaco against Bayern Munich. [GETTY]

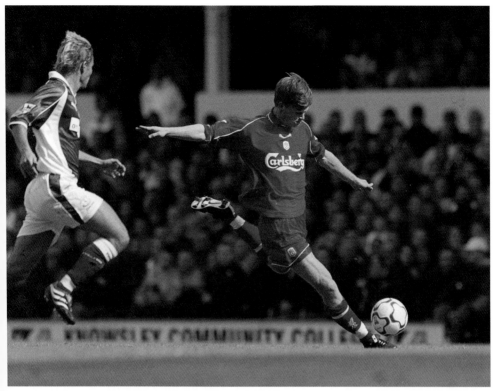

A thrilling start at Liverpool with goals against their greatest rivals, Everton and Manchester United in the space of a few weeks. [OFFSIDE]

My first serious trophy at Liverpool was the League Cup with a 2-0 victory over Manchester United. I marked David Beckham that day. [GETTY]

Celebrating another Steven Gerrard goal against Everton. [GETTY]

Early days with Norway in La Manga, Spain ahead of Euro 2000 [GETTY],
and then attempting to qualify for Euro 2004 against Spain in Madrid. [OFFSIDE]

The miracle of Istanbul. [OFFSIDE AND GETTY]

Scoring a crucial free kick against Chelsea in the 2006 FA Cup semi-final. [OFFSIDE]

The relief! Having missed my penalty in Istanbul, I just had to score against West Ham in the FA Cup final twelve months later. [GETTY]

The joys of being Craig Bellamy's teammate…
we put aside our differences and both scored in the Nou Camp in 2007. [OFFSIDE AND GETTY]

A challenging 18 months. Despair against Chelsea after scoring an own goal in the Champions League. Giving evidence against my former agent, Einar Baardsen. [GETTY]

Another goal, this one in the San Siro for Roma.
Later celebrating too with Francesco Totti, the club's icon. [GETTY]

Back in the Premier League with Fulham and facing Liverpool. [OFFSIDE]

Preparing for a Champions League game against Barcelona with APOEL Nicosia. I say preparing…
[GETTY]

Re-signing for my first club Aalesund in 2016 [GETTY]. This would bring me closer again to my brother.

Roberto Carlos is a legendary
left back and he was my manager at
Delhi Dynamos in India, a country
I would return to with Chennaiyin,
where the coach was Marco Materazzi.

THAT selfie with Khloe Kardashian.

Being dad.

Catching up in Liverpool with Steven Gerrard.

Being Norway's most capped player in history makes me very proud.

36

AFTER VICTORY IN THE CHAMPIONS LEAGUE, MY PLAY WAS SOLID when Norway held Italy 0–0 at Ullevaal in the beginning of June. I'm never pleased when I'm not on the winning side, and we could have won this match, but at the same time this was Italy, and after all we were Norway. We were still in the fight for second place, which would mean play-off matches and a chance to qualify for the World Cup in Germany the following summer. I was shown a yellow card after a half an hour, which meant that I had to miss the next qualifying match, Slovenia away. I was asked by our coach, Åge Hareide if I wanted to sit out the friendly against Sweden four days later in order to rest after a taxing season, but if there's one thing I don't like doing, it's resting when there's a match to be played. I wanted to play every match, every minute, all the time. In the absence of Martin Andresen and Claus Lundekvam, I was asked to captain Norway for the first time. I had waited a long time for this. Even though it was just a friendly, it felt huge to lead the team out at Råsunda. We hadn't won there since 1938.

It didn't start off well. Kim Källström gave Sweden the lead after barely a quarter of an hour with a rocket of a shot, but within the space of five minutes in the second half we levelled, and soon increased our lead to 3–1. I scored our first goal, like the captain should. It felt good, I have to say, captaining the squad, scoring and leading the team to a comeback against a regional rival, even if it was an insignificant victory. I take what I can get. Everything counts. I've always believed that.

I found a new agent based on a recommendation from Steven Gerrard. It was Struan Marshall, the same agent he used. And straight away he came to Liverpool to renegotiate my contract, and Benítez was so pleased with my efforts over the season that the club quickly agreed to an improved bonus agreement. I had two years remaining on the contract. It felt so good to be done with Baardsen.

With Struan Marshall, I was dealing with a real pro.

At the same time Benítez purchased a player from Middlesbrough, Boudewijn Zenden. In addition, both Harry Kewell and Stephen Warnock were available, so it was going to be a tough battle for a spot on my side. But I wasn't worried about Zenden, Kewell was often injured, and Warnock was not a threat. Benítez told the squad that he wanted to rotate the team more in the coming season. He had noticed that the team was not physically strong enough, and in addition to buying several players he had prepared an extra tough training plan for that summer. Just before the start of the Premier League, the *Daily Telegraph* asked its readers to select their dream team. The results were published on the opening weekend. The three players with the most votes were Frank Lampard, John Terry and Thierry Henry, but in tenth spot was me. I received the third most votes among defenders. It's not important. Well, maybe a little – as I've said, I take what I can get. Everything counts.

Back in Norway there were very different concerns. In the midst of all the newspaper articles about the Ferrari earlier that summer, I'd been contacted by a journalist from *Dagbladet* about a different rumour. As it happens, I was in the Ferrari on the way to training at Melwood. He said he'd heard talk about me sending texts to female celebrities, those were his words. He said he'd heard that there was talk of the same text message being sent to different women. I thought he was taking the piss, why was he calling me about this?

Let me start by saying that when on national-team duty the other players and I used to sit around bored at night. There are limits to how many computer games you can play. I read plenty of Henning Mankell but I'm not a big reader, and neither were the others. We couldn't go into town or there would be instant headlines in the tabloids. So, we sat there. Any entertainment proposals were welcomed. I'm the first to admit that it often took a rather childish turn, and I didn't exactly raise the bar. For example, Jan Gunnar Solli used to turn famous fairy tales into flirtatious tales, and as I said, we weren't exactly a discerning audience. And if he thought one of them was particularly good, we agreed to send it to someone. I mean, we were young – I was 24 that summer – we were totally immature, but above all, a lot of us were single. I think that's how it started. We had phone numbers of loads of women because as rich, young, professional footballers, you get quite a few offers. I wouldn't exactly say I was one of those who got the most numbers, that was probably John Carew, who was one of seven or eight of us to take part in it. I wasn't one of those who sent the most text messages, either, but I was one of several on the national team who did. And quite often we received replies. That was how it started, I think. Later I started sending text messages on my own, too. But these were genuine proposals to meet up for dinner or something. Happily, and much to my surprise, I got replies from some of them, too.

I was divorced. I lived alone in Liverpool and there were some long nights. I wrote some text messages, very innocent and maybe a little inept and naive, but I always said who they were from, obviously. Never anything else.

That was all I heard from the journalist. Time went by.

One day I was catching the plane home from Norway. Wednesday, 3 August. Newspapers lay on the passenger seats; nothing unusual about that. And then suddenly I saw my face on the front page. Lying on all the seats was an edition of Norwegian tabloid *VG* with me on the cover. The headline was about a passenger jet that had crashed, and as if that wasn't unpleasant enough on a plane, my ugly mug was also gaping at everyone: 'Famous women receive identical SMS: Reject Riise's chat-up lines!' in bold, blue type.

I opened the paper. There was a two-page spread. In large print: 'Celebrity women reveal SMS chat-up lines'. A large picture of me smiling accompanied the story, and around the article they had placed small headshots of famous women.

I could hardly comprehend what was written there. It was all about how I was meant to have sent an identical text message to 'dozens of famous ladies', according to information *VG* had apparently obtained. I felt like getting up, tearing the newspapers out of every single pair of hands of everyone else and shouting that it was all a lie, but I could do nothing other than sit there and endure the scowling looks of my fellow passengers for the duration of the flight. Two days later *Dagbladet* published something the paper must have spent the entire summer working on, a piece in the comment section that they billed as 'The Complete Riise SMS Story'. *VG* had beaten them to the punch. Yet this article, titled 'Anyone a Match for Me?' was, if possible, even more condescending and despicable. It mentioned fifteen Norwegian female celebrities who were 'victims' of my texts. That was not true.

First of all: a number of the women mentioned in the case, or who spoke out, I had never sent a text message to in my entire life. I didn't even know who several of them were. I don't know why they came forward, but some of them were not exactly publicity-shy. That said, let me be completely honest: I sent a lot of text messages. But it was over a period of almost a year, not in one spell like the papers made it appear. But I've always sent a lot of text messages. To all kinds of people, in all contexts. If someone has done something good, I try to remember to praise them. If someone has made a fool of themselves, like with a football referee, I might tweet about it. I have always been hyperactive; text messages and social media have been no exception. So yes, I'd sent text messages to quite a few of the women who were mentioned in the newspapers. A number of them had also replied. Over the course of the year maybe four of those mentioned had come to Liverpool, and we'd had a brilliant time together. Now they were singing a different tune.

One of those who spoke out was Pia Haraldsen, a TV presenter and journalist'. 'I was provoked to act due to John Arne's behaviour. Not only is it stupid and pathetic to do something like that but also terribly disrespectful.' I mean, I'd met her – she'd answered yes to my text with the offer of dinner for two at Hos Thea, a restaurant in Oslo's most affluent district, Frogner. But it had been a disaster, the entire dinner. It's the only time I've found an excuse to cut a date short. She wouldn't go into the restaurant until I opened the door for her. She wouldn't sit down until I pulled out her chair. She commented on the fact that I drank from my glass of water even though she hadn't had any of hers yet. The same thing happened when the food was served. She made me feel tiny. I later found out that she had been to a royal christening around that time: her stepfather was apparently the nephew of Queen Sonja or something like that – so maybe that was the reason. I thought it was strange that a grown woman who was driven to the date by her mum would behave like that.

Another person who spoke out was Marna Haugen, later known as the blogger Komikerfrue. She told the papers that she had let her now husband, the comedian Ørjan Burøe, pretend to be her and reply to me. But there were other things she didn't mention. For example she didn't describe how we met the first time. I went out for a bite to eat in Oslo. Suddenly I felt a hand grab my arse. I turned, but before I could see who it was, the woman pressed herself against me and kissed me. It was Marna Haugen. Not that I had anything against it. We were both single then, she was the former Miss Norway. And we dated for a while afterwards, and when I sent her a text, four months had passed, and I had no clue that she had got together with another guy in the meantime.

But I said nothing when the papers rang. All I could do was sit idly by and watch the case get blown completely out of proportion. The newspapers were having a field day that summer: first the Ferrari, then this. I felt like the boy in the schoolyard. And it just went on and on. Everyone who had thought that I was an idiot was reaffirmed in that belief. One feather becomes five hens. Soon the story grew to say that I had sent inappropriate pictures, but, I mean, these were the most innocent and awkward flirty texts. That was embarrassing enough, in the full glare of publicity. In the end I considered taking a break from the national team. Not because I didn't want to play, but I would run into Norwegian journalists, who no longer asked about anything other than these text messages. It no longer mattered that most of what was reported was a lie or heavily distorted. I rang Åge Hareide when it was at its worst and said, 'I don't know if I can take it anymore, I want to take a break.' I didn't know if I could take it anymore. Go to Norway? I would just be laughed at.

Even now when I walk down Karl Johan, the main street in Oslo, people shout at me: 'Send me a text, too!'

So I stop and ask for their number. And then I send a text. And sign off *SMS King*. Because that's me, after all. God, I was 24 years old and single. I just wanted to have fun.

Months later I stood by the window back home in Woolton. The summer of 2005 was over, and the autumn had arrived in Liverpool. The Ferrari was out in the courtyard. I looked out at it. It was October and rainy. I had spoken to my new advisor, Jan Kvalheim, the former beach volleyball player. He insisted that the car was bad for my public image. All the articles in the paper that summer proved it, he said, and I needed to sell it.

The drops gathered on the red paint. My entire life I had dreamed of this car. I had worked hard. I had been kicked and knocked down. I had endured pressure and dared to trust myself. I had taken the long walk from the halfway line to the penalty spot in a Champions League final, surrounded by 70,000 wild, screaming football fans and with the whole world watching on TV, placed the ball and breathed in.

Then this? The car was my reward, proof that I did not back down but stood up for myself and my team. The yellow and black logo rested on the bonnet, just like a shield. For five months I had owned that Ferrari.

I picked up the phone and rang the dealer. 'I need to sell the car.'

I still get cross when I think about it. I have absolutely no regrets about buying it but every fibre of my being regrets that I gave in and sold the car. It was admitting to the lads at Miller's that they were right. It was running away from the bullies.

But the only thing I could think was that maybe people would like me better if I sold it.

37

'You never drink coffee?'

'No, I don't like it. I'll have a hot chocolate instead.'

'It's a bit childish, isn't it?'

'Yeah, maybe, but it can't be helped. I order Caesar salad without dressing too, even though I know that means a Caesar salad without the Caesar. It doesn't bother me if things like that mean people think I'm ... I don't know what they think. I don't care. Some people react to the fact that my wife is in charge of what I wear, but those people are thick, they should have seen how I used to dress. I looked like a rainbow. An expensive rainbow...'

'What brand is your camel-hair coat?'

'Hugo Boss. It's nice, isn't it?'

'Yes, very elegant.'

'...'

'Should we talk a little about what you're doing at the moment?'

'Yes.'

'Where do you and Louise live, for example?'

'We live in a house on Slinningsodden back in Ålesund.'

'You're back where you grew up?'

'Yes. I can see the lights from the city centre across the bay at night, just like when I was little.'

'How does that feel?'

'Seeing the lights? ... The reason we moved there is because I was going to make my comeback at Aalesund in 2016 ... can we talk about that now or should we wait?'

'...'

'That didn't exactly go as I had imagined, but regardless, by the time I had retired

Louise had already opened a furniture shop in the centre with my sister-in-law. She was doing her thing, and now it was my turn to accommodate her work, like she had done for years with me. We do up flats pre-sale, as well.'

'You do up flats?'

'No, I'm the muscles. I carry furniture. I help her. We do a lot together, when I'm not off travelling. There's a fair bit of that. Among other things, I work for the betting company, Betsson – I'm what they call one of their ambassadors. I work as a tour guide, an MC and I take part in TV adverts and events all over. What else? A few times a year I play on a team called the Liverpool Legends, along with some of the greatest players in Liverpool history: Steven Gerrard, Jamie Carragher, Ian Rush, Bruce Grobbelaar, John Aldridge, Robbie Fowler and more. We travel round the world and play exhibition matches in front of packed stadiums, and the takings go to various worthy causes. It's great for me and I still have to pinch myself at the fact I'm getting to play with these big names.'

'But you're one of them, aren't you?'

'I'm not really able to think about it like that. I'm the ginger guy from Ålesund. I'm even living there again.'

'…'

'We played against the Real Madrid Legends at Anfield not long ago. Against people like Luís Figo, Clarence Seedorf and Roberto Carlos. My mum was there. She and Thormod came over for the weekend. Mum cried and I even arranged for her to meet Roberto Carlos. That was the last enjoyable thing we did together before we had a go at each other again on the phone.'

'How are the finances after all the trouble with Einar Baardsen and the debt you accrued?'

'I can't complain. I found out about the debt all the way back in 2005. It's a long time ago. I played three more seasons at Liverpool, three at Roma and three at Fulham and … I paid off the debt left by Baardsen as quickly as possible. 'I have tried to forget how long it took. I've put all the documents and the bills in the black box. But I settled the account. And I earned a lot of money after it was done, too.'

'But you drive to Oslo, you don't fly?'

'It's because of the dogs. Louise and I almost always go out together, and then we can't leave them behind.'

'What kind of dogs do you have?'

'We have two small dogs: Elita, who is a long-haired chihuahua, and Khloe, who is a small Pomeranian. It's named after one of Louise's big heroes: Khloe Kardashian. They only weigh six kilos in total.'

'So you take them for walks out on the point by the sea?'

'I'm sure that doesn't look very masculine...'

'You don't stay at a hotel when you're here, either?'

'We could have done. We prefer to stay with Louise's dad and stepmother in Ullevål. Next weekend we are going to celebrate my mother-in-law's seventieth birthday on the Oslo-Kiel ferry. A round trip. I like family, I'm like that. I don't really like boats but it'll be fine.'

'Doing up flats in Ålesund and playing legends matches in front of 80,000 people all over the world, it's like two different lives, wouldn't you say?'

'Oh, for sure. But we're not planning on staying here forever. I've got plans for the future.'

'What kind?'

'Become a manager. I want to get out in the world as a manager. The Liverpool academy asked me to go over. Rafael Benítez recently invited me to come to Newcastle to see how things work there. Claudio Ranieri has said the same thing.'

'What's the goal then?'

'Premier League. Back there. And eventually the national team.'

'What would make you a good manager?'

'The advantage I've got is that I've been in the game for so long that I've played under a lot of good managers. I'll need to have a team of people around me, obviously, who complement me and do the things I can't.'

'Do you think people can picture you as national-team manager?'

'No, I don't think so. Because they have a completely different image of me.'

'...'

'But the fact that people judge me and don't believe in me, that has never done anything other than inspire me. Not many people thought I was going to succeed as a professional footballer either, when I left Norway. Only I know what I can do.'

38

A SEASON THAT STARTED WITH ME BEING SELECTED FOR THE DREAM team by the readers of the *Daily Telegraph* in August 2005 again saw me among Liverpool's highest appearance-makers. The only players that featured more than me were Steven Gerrard, Jamie Carragher, Xabi Alonso, Sami Hyypiä, Djibril Cissé and our new keeper, Pepe Reina. I think you could say that I stepped up when faced with the new competition that Benítez had brought in. I disproved the predictions that my days at the club were numbered and I did it on the pitch. When the season was over, I had played more than all of the new challengers on my left side combined. From late October, we won ten league matches in a row and we didn't let in a single goal in nine of them. In the January transfer window, Christoph Daum at Fenerbahçe said that the Turkish champions were interested in me, but I had no plans to leave Liverpool. I wanted to play in the red jersey for the rest of my career if possible. I remember Rafael Benítez coming out of the dressing room one day and shouting at me on the practice ground: 'John Arne, call your agent. It's time for a new contract!' I was so happy. They offered me an extension until 2009 and a wage increase of £500,000 to £2.5million. There weren't a lot of negotiations on my part. I signed. Obviously.

I claimed that the penalty miss in Istanbul was forgotten, but that might not have been entirely true.

May, 2006: beaming sunshine. More than 70,000 in the stands. As captain, Steven Gerrard introduced everyone to Prince William before kick-off. Gerrard said our name and we shook the Prince's hand. This was the sixth and final occasion the FA Cup final was going to be played at Millennium Stadium. The following year, the new Wembley would be ready. The fans of both sides did everything they could to make the occasion magnificent. We were to meet West Ham and their supporters were nearly as loud as ours, expressing their enjoyment at the team's participation in a rare final. And they soon had even more to celebrate.

After 21 minutes West Ham took the lead following an unlucky own goal by Jamie Carragher. They then doubled their advantage a few minutes later. But this was truly a magical final. Djibril Cissé reduced the lead with an incredible volley, and nine minutes into the second half Peter Crouch nodded the ball down to Gerrard, and once again our captain put all of his weight into the shot and sent the ball screaming into the top corner. Two-all. Our fans went crazy behind the goal. We were on our way to turning the match around. That's what we thought, at least. After 64 minutes West Ham took the lead once more after a freak goal from Paul Konchesky, and from then on time flew by. The clock was already on ninety minutes when I got the ball from Gerrard on the left. I was struggling with cramp. It had been a long, hot afternoon, but I swerved the ball in anyway. Fernando Morientes lost the header, but the clearance bounced out. Again, the ball came towards Gerrard. He walloped it from thirty-five yards. God, what a goal. I raced after him and when I caught up to him, I held his face in my hands. I must have stared at him in confusion because it really was an unbelievable goal. 'I can't believe it. That was crazy. I can't believe it,' I babbled while I gaped at the happy mug I held in my hands.

In extra time it was West Ham with the best chances, but when the referee blew for full time, the score was still 3–3. It had been a tremendous recovery. Now the match was going to be decided on penalties. Then I felt it. The penalty miss in the Champions League final rested inside me. But I wasn't scared. All I wanted was to avenge myself. I wanted to prove to the throng of people surrounding us, to everyone who watched the match on television that I was a person that could handle pressure, that I was strong. I walked over to Benítez. 'I want to take one.'

'Ok,' he said, looked down at his sheet and made a note. 'You take number four.'

Didi Hamann was up first and he scored. Sami Hyypiä missed. Then Gerrard thumped the ball into the net. For West Ham Teddy Sheringham had scored, while both Bobby Zamora's and Konchesky's penalties had been saved by Pepe Reina. It was 2–1 to us and it was my turn. I quietly took those long steps down the pitch. I was almost as exhausted as I had been in Istanbul. But this time there was no doubt. I placed the ball, I took a few steps back to get a good run-up. I thought of Ariana, looked down at her name sewn into my shoe. Then I took off. And this time I did what I normally do. I hammered the ball into the net. That's it. Now Anton Ferdinand had to score from his penalty, otherwise the trophy was ours. Pepe Reina was fantastic and made another save. We were FA Cup winners. Gerrard lifted the cup that proved it. Fireworks exploded in the sky above us. The supporters were dancing and singing in the stands.

That was my fifth season at Liverpool. In the league, we finished third, just one point behind Manchester United and nine behind Chelsea, who won the league again. The previous season we had ended up in fifth place, 37 points off the summit. In that respect, after losing ground in each year since my debut season, we were firmly back on track.

39

A FEELING PERSISTED WHEN I REPRESENTED THE NATIONAL TEAM, and it grew stronger around the time of the commotion surrounding the text messages and the Ferrari and all of that. The NFF didn't like me. Why else would nobody call me up to hear my side of things? Why didn't they ring me and ask how I was doing?

I remember feeling very young when I was promoted to the men's national team. Back then I was inexperienced and insecure. The problem was that my sense of feeling young didn't lose its grip on me as the years went by and I took on a more important role on the team. I felt distrusted and disliked by the NFF. I was a good player so they had to have me on the team. They were only too happy to use my name and image. In the marketing for the national team my image appeared everywhere. They also knew that the journalists wanted me at press conferences, that I was a popular interviewee, among other things because I said the things that other people wouldn't say. I stood out and the heads of the association knew how to benefit from it. But the burden that came in the wake of that, I had to carry on my own. As a person they preferred to keep me at arm's length. I tried to approach them. Every year, for example, the they organised a children's day at Ullevaal Stadium, and even though children came from everywhere, most of all it was a way for the children of the NFF employees to meet the players. A fringe benefit. And every year I stood there at the end of the session, signing autographs after everyone else had left. I think it's important to encourage children, no matter who they are. I sign autographs for anyone who wants one. I could stand there for hours signing things. But as soon as those duties were performed, the heads of the association preferred that I disappear. I think there was something about their behaviour that reminded me of things I preferred to forget, early events that lay deep inside the black box.

When I said I pictured myself eventually becoming captain of the national team, I felt like they were laughing at me. Captain? You?

But I was not the only one not being taken care of by the NFF. Others had far more serious problems than me. For example, a lot of players knew that Claus Lundekvam was struggling with gambling and addiction problems. On the one hand I felt incredibly sorry for him. On the other hand we were working for Norway, we had a responsibility, which meant that I could get a little annoyed that he got up to such things, even though I realised that it was out of his control. And there were times I covered for him. I remember a time when he didn't turn up at a meeting one morning. We had to catch a bus to go to recovery training following a match the previous night. I popped up to his room and knocked on his door. When he finally opened, he was standing there naked, eating spaghetti bolognese from a takeaway box. He was completely gone. I don't know what he had taken.

'Dammit, Claus, you're supposed to be downstairs. The bus is leaving.'

He just replied with a distant 'uh'. So I walked into the room, called downstairs and said that Claus had overslept. I got him in the shower and helped him get dressed. When we got downstairs everyone must have seen it, or smelled it – his eyes were bright-red – but nobody said a thing.

Åge Hareide managed to change my mind. I continued playing for the national team. 'Show us that you can perform, accept the challenge,' he said. I love challenges and I didn't want to quit, even though the thought had crossed my mind. I wanted to play on the national team and I wanted to excel. Besides, I thought that I could win over the NFF if I just continued to give my all for the national team.

Fresh from winning the FA Cup, I went to Oslo to play a friendly against Paraguay at the end of May 2006. We dominated and should have won but it ended 2–2. After the match we had dinner at our hotel on Holbergs Plass. Several of the players had their wives and girlfriends with them. One of them was Jan Gunnar Solli. He had brought a date with him, Maria. I was sat across from her and we got to chatting. Afterwards a bunch of us went out and over the course of the night Jan Gunnar and Maria started to argue and I tried to calm them both down.

Five or six days later I ran into Maria by complete chance. I asked how things were.

'It's over, I think,' she said.

I called Jan Gunnar first, a few days later, to see if it was okay for me to ask her out. I believe you should be careful with things like that but he was completely fine with it. A few nights later – each of us with a group of friends – we went to a restaurant near to where she lived. She was a year older than me and worked as a nurse in a hospital.

The World Cup started in June, once again without us, this time in Germany. In qualifying we had defeated Slovenia away but lost at home in a terrible match against Scotland. Personally I don't know if I've ever played worse at international level. Still, with a little luck we finished second in our group behind Italy and made it through to a play-off against the Czech Republic in the late autumn of 2005, but we never were never close to beating them. It was a massive disappointment to miss out on yet another tournament with the national team. The only comfort was that England's national-team manager, Sven-Göran Eriksson, said that he would have selected me for his squad if I'd had an English passport.

In the summer, Benítez brought in the Brazilian Fábio Aurélio from Valencia, yet another challenger on my wing. In addition he bought Craig Bellamy from Blackburn Rovers. Bellamy, playing a completely different position on the pitch, would turn out to be more dangerous for me than Aurélio. But for the time being I trained hard, as always, and watched the World Cup matches. I followed England, obviously, and Australia. The latter first and foremost due to the fact that I was neighbours with Tim Cahill. He was one of the best players at Everton and star of the Australian national team. We were good mates. He had a boy who was two years older than Ariana. Occasionally I went over there just to hear the sounds of a child in the house. But I usually came over late at night, and of course Kyah was asleep by then. Tim and I had a fairly fixed ritual: Liverpool and Everton never played home matches on the same weekend. So every time the one who was playing an away match got home, we rang each other. Probably around half-eleven or twelve: 'Do you fancy popping by?'

Neither of us could sleep after matches. The adrenaline would still be pumping through the veins. So we met up, chatted and played pool or something, always with the TV on in the background. We talked about all kinds of things. There were little tricks that the home teams occasionally did to annoy the visiting opponent.

These were the kinds of things we could talk about. They would turn up the heat in the dressing room, for example. Only cold water in the showers. Air conditioning on full blast. And he had a Lamborghini, so cars were an interest we shared.

It's a strange life. But sleep wouldn't come. There was no point tossing and turning in bed all night. Not until five or six o'clock in the morning did I shuffle back across the square and go to bed.

Tim Cahill had a brilliant tournament. He scored Australia's first ever goal in a World Cup. Then he scored another right afterwards. I probably felt a little jealous.

40

FOR THE FIRST FRIENDLY OF THE SUMMER, I WAS PICKED TO CAPTAIN Liverpool. To run around with the armband and the Liverpool jersey on felt like an honour, even though it was only for one match in the middle of July against Wrexham. But anyway, at Liverpool I didn't have a hope in hell of becoming captain, like I did with the national team. At club level we had Steven Gerrard – Captain Fantastic – and there wasn't anyone in the world who could challenge him, but Benítez clearly wanted to remind me of my responsibilities at the club.

In the same match I first wore the armband', Craig Bellamy made his debut as a Liverpool player. His acquisition had been a surprise to us. He was known as a bit of a troublemaker. On the pitch he was loud-mouthed and arrogant. He constantly yapped at referees, opposing players and teammates alike. His mouth was going all the time, and the swearwords literally poured out of him. That was his playing style. He was irritating but it was his way to get the most out of his abilities.

He had this way of walking, I remember. He came to his first Liverpool training session with his chest out, always strutting about. And on the training pitch he got stuck in straight away. Such a tough talker: 'Fuck off. Shut the fuck up.' Non-stop: 'Fuck you. Fucking shit.' But he was all bark and no bite. We quickly discovered that. As soon as someone confronted him about his shit-slinging, he backed down. He was short, quite skinny. I laughed at him more than anything. All the things that came out of his mouth. I just laughed and if he went too far, I told him so: 'Shut the fuck up, you fucking midget.' I could do it, too.

But he was a good player, fast, and he could score. In his debut against Wrexham he scored his first goal for the club. We won 2–0. Otherwise our pre-season matches were poor, not least a 5–0 loss against Mainz in the final warm-up before the season. The fans were concerned, but we were hurting from all the training sessions.

For seven long weeks we had been at it. Running, lifting and sprinting. My test results had always been good but they were even better than ever. I felt good, calmer than I'd been in a long time. I had a lot of chats with Steven Gerrard and Jamie Carragher about my game. I was good at going forward on the pitch but sometimes struggled with my defensive play. That was my Achilles heel. I wanted to get better, and they helped me. We discussed and polished the details, talked about positioning in various phases of the opposing team's attack, considerations that constantly had to be made.

Maria moved in with me at the house in Woolton. It felt good. I'd got better at saying no to things. I was prone to follow every new impulse, but I had a newfound confidence. I was worse on my own, I knew that. I was unhappy being single. I quickly got insecure and made stupid decisions. I missed Ariana, obviously. She was five and a half now and lived with her mum in Ålesund. But in a way I also felt more present. Secure. I hadn't felt that way for some time. I had rid myself of Einar Baardsen and hired Struan Marshall, something that meant a big weight had been lifted off my shoulders. The debt was being paid off, and the texts and the Ferrari were memories that were safely stored away in the black box. It's the same feeling you get when you put on a freshly-ironed shirt, or when you know exactly what time it is.

On 13 August we met Chelsea in the Community Shield, the match that had been known as the Charity Shield when I started my career at Liverpool five years earlier. Since Wembley was still under construction, the match was again held at Millennium Stadium in Cardiff. Chelsea had won the league and we had won the FA Cup the previous season.

Though the pre-season had been poor, I was going to charge out of the blocks at full speed this season.

Seven or eight minutes into the match Chelsea got a corner. It was easily headed out and I gathered the ball on the edge of our penalty area and ran with it. As I raced ahead, I looked for someone to pass to. I considered crossing it to Jermaine Pennant, who I saw waving his arms on the opposite side, but it was never really an option. I was going to do this on my own. I noticed John Terry backing away, so I just continued running straight ahead. I had held the ball for a long time now, nearly ten seconds. I was in the middle of their half, then ran a little more before I struck the ball with a straight instep. It went in. It was a dream goal.

Only a few days later I found out that Chelsea and José Mourinho had asked if I was for sale. I was not.

In the league opener we faced newly-promoted Sheffield United. Even playing away, it was a team we were expected to beat. We only managed a draw, but even worse for me personally was the way I twisted my left ankle after 23 minutes of play. My first thought was that it was broken, it hurt so much when I tried to stand on it. Soon they brought the stretcher over and carried me off the pitch. Luckily there was no fracture, but with three strained ligaments I had to rest for three weeks. So much for my flying start.

I was forced to miss the first two international qualifiers for the European Championship in Austria and Switzerland but I stayed with the squad all the same. I wanted to be there. I couldn't stand the thought of lying at home in Liverpool. Liked or not by the NFF, I was dedicated to the national team. In our first two games we beat Hungary 4-1 away from home and then beat Moldova 2-0 at home. In a manageable group, reaching a majour tournament felt achievable.

In the league. I came back against Everton for the Merseyside derby. We were down 3-0 when I was brought on in the 64th minute. I twisted my ankle again and had to go off. Another two weeks on the sidelines. But I returned against Tottenham, the day before my 26th birthday. Finally our play was flowing. My goal to make it 3-0 at the close of the match was the icing on the cake. A shot from around forty yards went low and to the keeper's left corner. 'Even by his standards it's a special goal,' declared the TV commentator. I was back. And sitting in the stands was Maria.

Our play was erratic all autumn; good at home but poor away. But we more or less kept up with the leaders and I usually started at left-back. I scored again with a long-range shot in the League Cup against Reading, when we won 4-3. When we beat Fulham 4-0 in early December we had gone 25 home league games without defeat. I had recently got engaged.

Not everyone felt as calm, obviously. Craig Bellamy had been forced to skip training sessions and matches because of a court case where two women accused him of assault outside a Cardiff nightclub, a fresh incident. But after five days in court he was acquitted. To be honest, I didn't think much about the case he was involved in. If anything I felt bad for him. Being famous, football players can get quite a lot of stick when they're out, but of course it's just a matter of walking away, getting the doormen to take care of things.

In December, the draw for the first knockout round of the Champions League was announced. We were training at Melwood when the equipment manager came running over. 'Barcelona!' he shouted. 'We've drawn Barcelona!' We were going to meet the reigning champions. We had won our group, and the thinking was probably that we would face easier opposition ahead, but Barcelona had ended up behind Chelsea in their group, and so instead of drawing Celtic, Porto or Lille, we got them. The first match was to be played at Camp Nou. No English team had won there since John Toshack hit the only goal in a UEFA Cup tie there for Liverpool in 1976. Thirty-one years had passed. I didn't think about that. Instead I reminded myself how the previous year we had drawn Benfica, supposedly easier opposition, and lost. Maybe this would go better.

The week after the draw we held our Christmas party. Like every year the invitation stated that it was a costume party. A number of clubs have turned their Christmas parties into fancy-dress balls, all to make the festivities something other than a booze-up. Craig Bellamy came dressed as a psychopathic joker, I remember, while I had found a Shrek costume online. Luis García came as a pimp, Steven Gerrard was a punk and Robbie Fowler was Saddam Hussein. Peter Crouch came as a parrot, Jerzy Dudek as Darth Vader and Daniel Agger as Elvis. Dirk Kuyt was Superman, Jamie Carragher Spiderman, and Sami Hyypiä came as Zorro. At Liverpool things were pretty harmless for the most part. Circumstances were tougher at Fulham, when I went there some years later. We had to draw slips of paper to decide what we were going to dress up as. I still have memories of players dressed in a G-string, wearing nothing else, images that are impossible to erase. Where's the black the box when you need it?

41

I LOVED PLAYING FOR THE NATIONAL TEAM. I WAS ALLOWED TO PLAY more of a free role than I played for my club, and I enjoyed being able to surge up the wing, and I often tried my luck with a shot. If I was asked to play, I turned up. No matter how cold and uncaring the NFF were towards me, I never said no to anything they asked. I travelled with the national team even when I was injured. I asked to play in the friendlies when the coaches wanted to rest me. The national team was extremely important to me. I'd been abroad for so long that the gatherings eased any feeling of homesickness.

But after international matches, the Norwegian pundits usually complained that I hadn't dominated play. Even when they wrote that I was good, they might wonder why I hadn't controlled the match to a greater degree. They seem to have forgotten that I played at left-back. Another usual complaint from Norwegian journalists was that my play didn't flow as well on the national team as at Liverpool. That should be obvious. Firstly, I had better players around me at club football, that's just how it was, and in addition we trained together daily, not just for two or three days at some point in the year. Sometimes I was under enormous pressure because I was a player who was expected to take hold of the game, make things happen, something that was not required of me at Liverpool.

There was nothing I wanted more than to give something back to the national team and help give our fans a place in the European Championship or the World Cup. With a spot in qualifying Group C for the European Championship in 2008, I thought we had our best chance in a long time. But after a fine start to qualification, we lost to Greece in Athens in the final match before the winter break and then at home against Bosnia-Herzegovina in the first international of 2007. Unlike in previous campaigns, we were able to raise ourselves back up, and at the interval of our next game four days later against Turkey we led 2–0. We'd played well. This was a result that would give us an enormous lift on the way to the European Championship. Because of the behaviour of their fans, the match was played in Frankfurt. But we soon discovered that there are a lot of Turkish people living in Germany. We were close to accomplishing something special. Then our keeper, Thomas Myhre, made a massive blunder: 2-1. Then – in the final minute – sure as hell he made another one. He managed to let a free-kick slip through his fingers and sneak under him: 2–2. God, I was furious. It was such unbelievably poor goalkeeping. Thomas is a good guy, so I wouldn't think of telling him off, but I doubt that I was able to hide my disappointment and annoyance. I more than anyone know that mistakes can happen on a football pitch, but this should have been our victory. With average goalkeeping we would have been in a good position to finally reach a tournament with the national team. It ruined such a good match and it was fucking awful, to be honest. It was tough to swallow.

42

BARCELONA. LAST SIXTEEN OF THE CHAMPIONS LEAGUE.

We crashed out of the domestic cups over the course of two evenings in January 2007. Both times it was Arsenal who were too strong for us. Both home defeats.

The last match before Barcelona was against Newcastle on 10 February. After an early goal by Bellamy, it was 1-1 with twenty minutes remaining when I brought down Steven Taylor in the penalty area. We lost, we were out of the cup competitions and were definitely out of contention for the league, again, and this time I was to blame. I was so disappointed in myself. I saw Stevie shout something at me. I couldn't hear him but he was fuming. Of course he was, but in that exact moment I couldn't take a telling-off, even though it was deserved. 'Fuck off!' I shouted back. In the dressing room he came straight over to me and stood in front of my spot: 'Is it like that now? Telling me to fuck off?'

I knew my place. He was our captain. I was silent, I stared at my shoes. 'No,' I said. 'Sorry. I'm sorry.'

'All right,' he said. 'Don't let it happen again.'

'I won't,' I said.

In the next match I was up against Ronaldinho and Barcelona at the cavernous Camp Nou. The club had been sold to two American investors, Tom Hicks and George Gillett, which would soon cause a lot of unrest. A new defender was brought in, Álvaro Arbeloa, who had grown up in Real Madrid's B team. I had just made a fool of myself in front of our captain. I felt calm amongst mounting pressure.

43

THE TEAM TRAVELLED TO THE ALGARVE TO RECHARGE FOR THE match against Barcelona. We had to get away from the English weather. We needed fresh energy. For five days we were going to do some light training, play golf, relax in the sun and socialise. That was the plan.

We stayed at Barringtons Golf and Spa hotel, which was located in an exclusive resort called Vale do Lobo. I shared a room with Daniel Agger.

On Thursday it was decided that we should have a team dinner without the trainers and managers. At these dinners the players were allowed to have a beer or two, something I never took advantage of. Even though there were six days before the match, I thought the most professional thing to do would be to abstain. But a couple of beers wasn't going to hurt anyone else. If only they had managed to stick to a couple.

Steven Gerrard had called the owner and booked a private room for us at Monty's Restaurant and Bar. He was familiar with the area having played a lot of golf there. Monty's was situated in an area near the beach, where there were lots of other bars, restaurants, along with several pools and private security. They served good fish and chips, we were told, but I preferred steak. The interior was black and white, with matching tiles on the floor, and I remember seeing a karaoke machine in the bar. There were glass walls separating our area of the restaurant, so the other guests could see us, not that it mattered.

A couple of the lads started drinking before the food arrived. Among them was Craig Bellamy. Pretty soon a microphone appeared on the table. And Bellamy bellowed into it: 'Riise's gonna sing! Riise's gonna sing!' He started before the food was served and continued while we ate. He was already quite drunk and I was already quite annoyed.

After we had eaten, we joined the other guests. There were not enough seats for everyone, so some of us had to stand. Pretty soon Bellamy was over by the karaoke machine with the microphone in the hand: 'Riise's gonna sing! Next on stage is Riise! Riise's gonna sing!'

I'd had enough. Furious, I went over to him: 'I'm not singing. Shut the fuck up or else I'm gonna smash you!'

He screamed back: 'I'm gonna fucking kill you, you ginger cunt!'

The other lads looked at us. Steven Gerrard was sitting there, so too were Jamie Carragher and Sami Hyypiä. Bellamy shut up, and I left with Hyypiä – who was just getting a little tipsy – and got a taxi back to the hotel. Agger hadn't wanted to leave yet, so I promised to leave the door unlocked. Back in the room I fell asleep almost immediately. It was no later than half twelve.

I woke in the dark to hear keys jingling and someone opening the door. Obviously I thought it was Agger who had switched on the light. I turned, but my eyes were half-asleep, and I didn't see anything in the sudden, bright glare. But something made me realise that it wasn't Agger. And soon I could see him – Craig Bellamy at the foot of my bed with a golf club in his hands. The golf club was one of his own. He must have grabbed it from his room. Steve Finnan, who shared a room with Bellamy, was there too, but he just stood there. Bellamy raised the club over his head and swung as hard as he could. He tried to hit my shins, which most likely would have ended my career, but I managed to pull my leg away in time. I jumped out of bed, pulled off the sheet, and held it between us like I was some kind of half-awake matador. Bellamy sputtered: 'Nobody disrespects me like that in front of the lads!' He was completely gone. I didn't know if he was just drunk, or if he had taken something else. 'I know who I am. I don't care if I go to jail! My kids have enough money for school and everything. I don't care. I'll fucking do you!' He raised the club and swung again. This time he connected. Full force on my hip. I was so pumped with adrenaline that I didn't feel the pain, but he hit me hard. It was an iron. Number four, I think. The next blow smashed into my thigh. I tried to hold up the sheet, but he continued to strike. He could seriously injure me. At the same time, I knew I could take Bellamy if I needed to. I was bigger and stronger. Finnan stood by the door. Maybe he was there to stop Bellamy if it got too bad, but he was short and skinny. He wouldn't have stood a chance once I made my mind up. However, I knew that if I responded to Bellamy's attack, my career at Liverpool would be over, and I didn't want to be remembered as the guy who beat up a teammate. All things considered, I'm not much of a fighter. It's not my style. But I was under pressure. I tried to calm him down: 'Put down the club and let's fight with our fists. Put down the club and let's sort things out the old-fashioned way. Come on! A proper fight!'

He just stood and glowered at me for a while. Then he said: 'Tomorrow at nine o'clock we'll meet and finish this.' Then he left.

I checked the clock. Almost three. A lot of things had happened that night; I didn't know about most of it because I'd gone to bed early, but when I looked out the window to see what all the racket was about, I saw the flashing lights of a police car and our keeper, Jerzy Dudek, being bundled into the back in handcuffs. He was singing and pounding on the roof of the car. That kind of behaviour wasn't like him.

I rang the doctor and asked him to come up and take a look at me. Already my hip and thigh were turning black and blue. After taking care of my injuries, the doctor called Benítez. I don't know if he was asleep or if he'd been up waiting for the players. He hurried upstairs and his shock was palpable when he entered the room. I think he must have realised what had happened straight away. But he didn't say much. He was the same as always, calm and controlled. He just mentioned that everyone involved would meet up the next day for a chat. Then he left, first to demand a report from Gerrard about who in the world had let things spiral out of control that night.

When Agger returned to our room and found out what Bellamy had done, he completely snapped. I had to restrain him keep him from going after him.

I tried to sleep but sleep wouldn't come. In the morning I got up, showered and examined the injuries in the mirror. Calmly, I got myself ready. At five to nine I left the room. Agger wanted to come with me. I found Bellamy's door and knocked. No answer. I knocked again, still with no sign of movement inside. Was that a sound? It was nine o'clock. I was ready. I knocked again, but nobody opened. For ten minutes, we waited outside. Then Agger and I went to have breakfast instead. The rumours of what had happened during the night had clearly spread. The lads sat there, laughing amongst themselves. After a while Bellamy showed up. He must have stayed quiet as a mouse in his room while I stood outside his door. He didn't even glance at me. He grabbed some food and sat down. Not a sound. Nothing. Dudek arrived with scrapes on his face. The lads laughed even more.

And the sniggering continued at the training session. It was just light training to sweat the alcohol out, for those who needed to. Plenty of us had red eyes and heavy heads. I didn't like that they just laughed about it. One of our teammates had attacked me and could have ended my career. I mean, what happened to supporting each other? Why did nobody challenge him about it? But they must have thought that this was a private matter between Bellamy and me. I suppose they were right. I would probably have done the same. I felt like knocking him out. I would have been justified in giving him a pounding but I had too much respect for Benítez and the team. We were about to play an important match. There was enough commotion as it was. Bellamy apologised but not on his own initiative, only when he was more or less forced to by the manager. He had no choice and hoped maybe an apology would lessen the punishment that awaited. He ended up with an £80,000 fine. I received no punishment, contrary to the reports of some journalists.

I get that some people can't handle their alcohol, that they become the worst version of themselves, but if you're an adult, you ought to know when to stop drinking. There were others who got drunk that night, like Sami Hyypiä, for example, without behaving like idiotic teenagers because of it. They drank, calmly and like adults. When Bellamy tried to blame it on booze, like he did, most of all I think it's very weak.

44

BARCELONA TOOK THE LEAD AT CAMP NOU BARELY A QUARTER OF AN
hour in, Deco nodding in a glancing header, triggering cheers from more than
90,000 fans in the stands. They had us under pressure, and there was a feeling that
everything could unravel for us after the Spaniards' early goal. Frank Rijkaard had
assembled an impressive team. Not only did he have the world's best player at the
time, Ronaldinho, but also a brilliant young talent named Lionel Messi.

Benítez was a flawless tactician, something he demonstrated by selecting both
Craig Bellamy and me for the team despite what had happened and the insane
media pressure that followed with it. He must have thought that we had a lot to
prove. I stood there before the match, still bruised from the other night.

We braced ourselves.

Two minutes before the break Craig Bellamy equalised. It was a fantastic feeling.
We had now drawn level with Barcelona away. Bellamy celebrated by running
towards the corner flag, where he stopped and made a swinging motion, like he was
holding a golf club. I thought it was fucking disrespectful. He'd attacked me with an
iron. For me it was more than just an amusing gag. The celebration also revealed the
sincerity of his apology.

Then, deep into the second half, with barely a quarter of an hour remaining,
Dirk Kuyt was played through by Gerrard, but his first touch took him too too close
to Barcelona goalkeeper Víctor Valdés to score. Rafael Márquez – my old teammate
from Monaco – tried to head the ball out of danger but only got the ball as far as
Bellamy. Instead of shooting, he saw that I was wide open and centred the ball across
the penalty area. Even with my wrong foot I managed to get the ball in the net, over
the defender guarding the line.

People have made a lot of it. Afterwards he ran towards me and jumped up on me to celebrate the goal. Obviously we were euphoric, but that's exactly it – in a moment like that you don't think, you're just beside yourself with joy. But what we proved, both Bellamy and myself, was that we had the ability to use adversity to succeed on the pitch. We handled the pressure and distinguished ourselves in one of the biggest matches you can play, away to Barcelona in the Champions League. After the scandal and speculation we were the two goalscorers. Speaking to the press afterwards I said: 'I think fate would have it that both of us scored. Bellamy and I have had some issues before the match, but we put those behind us when it really mattered. His celebration, I don't mind. Listen, he's had a tough time too, and I realise it meant a lot to him. I'm happy for him and so is the team.'

But we could never be friends. I wanted to be the bigger man, but this was difficult to forgive.

Bellamy was sold at the end of the season. The club thought there was too much trouble around him. And we later played against each other, first when he was at West Ham, then when he was back at Liverpool and I was at Fulham. I always played all out against him. I obviously didn't try to injure him, but made I hard tackles, right on the edge, so he'd know how painful it was to face me – and never forget it. I remember one time Clint Dempsey went into a duel and the referee whistled for a foul, then Bellamy came charging over, as usual. Puffed out his chest. Yapping and swearing. Dempsey took one look at him and said: 'Do you wanna fight?'

Then Bellamy did what he always did when he wasn't full of Dutch courage, he shuffled off. Dempsey would have murdered him.

My decision in the hotel room was sensible. I mean, the two of us were dads. But the feeling has stuck with me all this time. I should have stood up for myself. Steven Gerrard once said to me a while back: 'If I'd been in your shoes, I don't think I would have managed.'

45

WE HAD DEFEATED BARCELONA, THE PREVIOUS YEAR'S CHAMPIONS League winners, 2–1. And I was the one who had scored the winning goal. And with my right foot! It is the only goal I've ever scored with my right foot. It's true. I scored one goal in my entire career with the wrong foot. The winning goal against Barcelona, away. Not too shabby.

Half an hour after the referee whistled for the end of the match, I could still hear the travelling supporters singing my song in the enormous, nearly empty stadium, their voices having gone hoarse a while ago:

John Arne Riise
I wanna know-ow-ow
How you scored that goal!

The fact that we lost 1–0 at home to them two weeks later didn't matter. We advanced on the away-goals rule. In the quarter-final we comfortably beat PSV Eindhoven, 3–0 in the Netherlands and then 1–0 at Anfield.

Chelsea were next in the semi-final.

They were out for revenge. Losing to us in the Champions League in 2005 stung. They dominated at home in England, they had won the Premier League two years in a row, yet we were the ones who could adorn ourselves with a Champions League title, not Chelsea. This would also be their third semi-final in four years. Their previous two appearances at this stage had ended in defeat.

Like two years earlier, the first match of the semi-final was to be played in London. We were soon under intense pressure. Pepe Reina made a fantastic save from a shot from Frank Lampard from barely ten yards out. Didier Drogba nearly found Joe Cole unmarked in our penalty area, and was then close to nodding in the opening goal himself. It looked like it would only be a matter of time before we capitulated, and after a half-hour our resistance broke. Their central defender Ricardo Carvalho sent a long ball up to Drogba, who spun away from Daniel Agger, before sending in a perfect ball that Joe Cole slid into the goal.

Going forward we couldn't manage anything. Early in the second half Craig Bellamy was substituted in favour of Peter Crouch, and our attacking game quickly picked up. But we were unable to score. I remember Agger being angry and upset in the dressing room afterwards because he had been fooled by Drogba before the goal. But it's like that being a defender. Sometimes you get caught out.

Against Chelsea at Anfield we got the first proper chance of the match. Steven Gerrard took a free-kick from the left but instead of hitting the ball towards the far post he centred to Daniel Agger. My Danish friend had clearly decided to get his revenge. He hammered the ball into the bottom corner: 1–0.

After the interval we had three big chances to take the lead on aggregate. One of them after I made a long, pinpoint cross that Dirk Kuyt got hold of with a brilliant header. Unfortunately it slammed into the crossbar. At the same time we had to guard against Chelsea's dangerous attacks. If they scored one goal, we would have to finish with three in order to advance to the final. But there were no more goals, neither after full time nor after extra time. Penalties. I remember smiling. We were a team that came up big when important matches were decided from the penalty spot. The final in the Champions League, obviously, and the FA Cup the previous year.

Chelsea scored just one of their three kicks.

We converted all of ours.

I drove through Liverpool in the evening darkness, pumped with adrenaline. The songs of our supporters still ringing in my head. I drove out to Woolton. We were bloody well in the Champions League final, I thought, and pounded my hands against the steering wheel in celebration. Back at the house I parked the car and let myself in. Dark and quiet. Maria had already gone to bed.

I always tried to differentiate between my life as a footballer and as a family man, tried to use my home to be like everyone else, to disconnect and feel normality seep in like a kind of therapy. But coming back to a quiet house after a big victory like a semi-final in the Champions League almost felt lonelier than after a loss.

That night it wouldn't have been fair to shuffle over to Tim's place and sit there watching TV and chatting. But I couldn't sleep either, it was impossible. I'd just be tossing and turning in bed. So I sat up, without switching on the lights. The TV was on. I watched highlights of the semi-final I had taken part in a few hours earlier, and when the news broadcast was over, I changed channels. I don't know if Maria realised I was sitting there. Guri never did either, because the same scenario had played out when we were married. In that respect I could sense that they diminished the joy I got from winning. At least, we didn't share that joy. With Louise it would be different, she loved to watch my matches. She enjoyed the victories with me and could joke around and put me in good mood after a loss. But during my time at Liverpool, and later at Roma, it wasn't like that. I came home, so geared up and happy after having put my laces through a free-kick against AC Milan or decided a match against Juventus three minutes into injury time, and the person I lived with just shrugged her shoulders. But maybe they didn't understand how huge football was to me. It saved me as a kid, it was all I had back then. It still meant everything to me. Maybe it was too much to ask them to watch.

46

THIS TIME THE FINAL WAS HELD IN ATHENS, AND IT WAS STRANGE. It was impossible to compare it to our first Champions League final. It wasn't nearly as big. It's sad to think back on it now, that I wasn't able to appreciate the insane fact that I was in my second final of the greatest of all club tournaments, but I wasn't. I wasn't able to grasp the amazing thing about the situation, that I was making history as the only Norwegian to take part in two finals, that I wasn't just sitting on the bench, but was one of the starting eleven in both. Because it's one thing to win trophies, but for me it means a lot that I actually played a part in writing the full story, left my mark on it. But it's only in hindsight that I'm able to see this. Back then there were football matches to be won. I didn't stop to look at what I had actually achieved. I just trained and played, match after match. I regret that today but maybe it wasn't possible to do it any different way. Maybe I'd be terrified to view all of this from the outside. I had to prepare for it like any other match. That was the only way I could perform.

We faced AC Milan, like the previous time. But in contrast to then we actually played well. We deserved to win this match. I had friends in the stands. Maria was there. I'd heard there had been huge chaos regarding the tickets before the match. There were loads of fake tickets in circulation and a lot of fans with genuine tickets were refused entry by Greek police outside the Olympic Stadium on the grounds that the arena was already full, even though it wasn't. The capacity was 74,000 people and only 63,000 got in to see the final.

For the entire first half we pressed and created chances. Immediately before the break Milan got a free-kick outside our penalty area, right in front of goal. Andrea Pirlo took it. He didn't hit it cleanly. The ball was headed for Pepe Reina's corner, and he would have caught it with little problem. But then – on its way – the ball struck Filippo Inzaghi on the arse, changed direction and bounced into the middle of the net, past a bewildered Reina who had thrown himself in the direction of the initial shot. Inzaghi celebrated like a madman, of course he did, who can blame him, but I thought he made it look as though he had done something fantastic. All he did was get hit in the arse.

We were down 1–0, undeservedly so, but in the second half we continued to press. Gerrard had a big chance after an hour of play. A mistake by Gattuso left him alone in front of Dida but he didn't get much power on his shot. Milan for their part barely had the ball but they defended well as always. We moved round and round outside their penalty area, hunting for an opening. But then Milan counterattacked. Kaká ran up the pitch with the ball, found Inzaghi with a through ball and this time it was a first-class goal by their striker. He coolly rounded Reina and rolled the ball into the net. There were eight minutes left and we were down 2–0. One minute before time we cut the lead on a corner by Kuyt, but this was Milan's victory. And maybe that was okay, at least in hindsight. When the referee blew the final whistle, it didn't really feel okay. But when I think back now, maybe Milan deserved to win the final in Istanbul and we deserved to win this one. So in a way things evened out. That's what I try to think. But it's never okay to lose any match.

In the league we had finished in third place, just like the previous year. It was a strong position but the demand for success is great at a club like Liverpool. Perhaps the worst thing was that the feeling that we were on the right track, that we were getting closer to the top teams, was gone. The previous year we'd ended up just one point off second place, nine points behind the winners. This year Chelsea and Manchester United swapped positions at the top, but we couldn't stay with them. This time there was a long drop to third place – we finished 21 points behind United, and fifteen points behind Chelsea in second place. All right, we played in our second Champions League final in three years, but when all is said and done we had to count the cups at the end of the season: zero.

47

AT THE BEGINNING OF JUNE, NORWAY WERE SET TO MEET MALTA AND Hungary at Ullevaal in the final two internationals before the summer holidays. After the blunders in the match against Turkey in Frankfurt, Thomas Myhre was not selected for the squad again. Football can be brutal. However, another player was selected. My brother. And not only was he picked for the squad, he was picked to start. Naturally I was over the moon. In many ways it a dream come true, two Riises playing together. But to be completely honest, his selection made me worry even more. He had previously played in a friendly against Serbia in Belgrade. He'd come on with less than thirty minutes remaining. I was almost crippled with anxiety. I could barely play, I followed everything he did on the pitch with concern. And it was just a friendly. These were the decisive European Championship qualifying matches. Bjørn was my little brother, after all. Obviously I knew how great he was, I'd say he was a better player than me in many ways, but he didn't have the same kind of flow in decisive moments. I wanted him to succeed so badly, so that everyone would realise what a fantastic player he was. No bad luck and no blunders. These things can happen to anyone on a football pitch, and as I said, things hadn't always flowed smoothly for him. I was terrified at the thought of him making a mistake that could destroy his career, or that something would happen that people could torment him about. Something I couldn't protect him from.

We shared a room at the hotel. I tried to tease him as much as possible so that he didn't have a chance to get nervous, but I would say that it was mostly to keep my own thoughts at bay.

Like most of the things I worried about, this too was completely wasted. Bjørn played brilliantly. The whole team did. We won both matches by a clear margin: 4-0.

48

THE MOST IRRITATING PLAYER I'VE PLAYED AGAINST? IF BY IRRITATING you mean the best, it's either Cristiano Ronaldo or Lionel Messi, while Zlatan Ibrahimović is not far behind. Strong as an ox. So bloody cocky and arrogant on the pitch, but of course he has every reason to be. Who can blame him?

But even though Ronaldo and Messi were the most complete players, it wasn't the technicians who gave me the greatest problems on the pitch. For me it was often an advantage that they wanted the ball at their feet before they raced off. So I could just stick close to them and spoil the chance. I struggled more with speedy wingers who loved to run into space behind you. I didn't have the speed of Arsenal's Theo Walcott, for example, or Aaron Lennon when he played at Tottenham.

The funniest in the dressing room was probably Peter Crouch. The body language alone of this 6ft 7in beanpole of a man was great entertainment. In addition to this he was always in a good mood, and very good at telling stories. Dirk Kuyt was funny because he spoke such strange English. Robbie Fowler didn't take himself too seriously and was a constant source of pranks; classic locker-room gags that nobody other than a footballer would get, and sometimes not even then. Hide the new guy's clothes so that he had nothing to change into when they came out of the showers. Maybe cut them into shreds. Fill his smelly socks with underwear, making them into small weapons to swing at someone. Those kinds of things.

Most irritating would probably have to be Craig Bellamy. As for the dirtiest, I don't know. Some guys would pinch you in the balls when the referee wasn't looking, or 'accidently' step on your toes. Some players would verbally taunt instead, using insults such as 'fat fuck'. After they'd knocked you down and been punished with either a yellow or a red card, they'd smile and say 'Got ya.' A lot of people get up to those kinds of things. If I had to pick one player, I'd probably have to mention myself. I'm very annoying to play against. I'm not proud of all the things I've done, but I've never shied away from using any means – just about – to win a match. That said, I've never set out to deliberately injure someone. There are players who are like that, but I'm not going to name them.

49

THE SUMMER OF 2007 WAS THE SUMMER OF BIG BUYS. FERNANDO Torres, Ryan Babel, Lucas and Yossi Benayoun for £65.3million altogether. It would seem the new American owners were serious when they said that they would spend in order to put Liverpool on an equal footing with clubs like Chelsea and Manchester United. But things were also different. When the chairman David Moores sold his shares in February, his family had owned the club for more than fifty years. Already during the first autumn with the new owners, we began to realise that there was friction between them and our manager, Rafael Benítez. But what concerned me more directly, was that the newspapers wrote that Benítez was interested in the Argentinian left-back Gabriel Heinze. My first reaction was that it sounded strange. He had played three seasons at Manchester United and would hardly be welcomed with open arms by our fans. In addition he was two years older than me; he had just turned 29. I tried to put the speculation out of my mind. I reminded myself that these kinds of rumours were part of the game, and that they always cropped up around big clubs. I was better than Heinze. Still, there was a nervousness that seeped into the calm I had carried around ever since I'd tossed Baardsen out on his arse, got my finances under control and started working with Struan Marshall nearly two years earlier. I wasn't quite able to shake off the feeling that the manager might not think I was good enough after all. The fact that he's considering other players for your position, that's not a positive sign. Heinze never came to Liverpool but went to Real Madrid.

Regardless the autumn didn't proceed exactly as planned. More and more often I was left on the bench. Arbeloa played left-back. He started all the matches, and Benítez praised him in the newspapers for the way he had established himself in the team. There were indications that Fábio Aurélio was also preferred over me at the back. Then, as if that wasn't bad enough, the young, untried Argentinian defender Sebastián Leto took my spot for the Champions League clash against Olympique Marseille on 3 October at Anfield. I was in shock. It was a scandal. I didn't understand what Benítez was up to. It could have been the feud he carried on with the owners – the rumours were buzzing that he was in danger of getting the boot, and he started to make some strange decisions. He became more and more obsessed with using his 'own' players, that is, the ones he had bought. But Leto was just a young lad, and he didn't do particularly well either. He played three matches more over the course of the season, before he disappeared to play in Greece.

We lost 1–0 to Marseille and after two matches in the Champions League we had scraped together one point. It got even worse when we lost to Beşiktaş in Istanbul during the next group match. As the previous year's runners-up, we were in serious danger of dropping out at the group stage. Finally – even after big victories at home against both Beşiktaş and Porto – we needed to beat Marseille in the final match in the south of France. Everything indicated that Benítez's job also hinged on the outcome of the fixture. As well as millions of pounds, of course.

I have a picture of Ariana on the windowsill. I can't remember where the name came from when we were expecting her. I'd wanted to have international names for my children, which can be pronounced both in Norwegian and in English, because we were going to be moving around. That's the way I thought. Ariana, Emma and Patrick. But then things happened. I ended up being the one who moved around, without them. Ariana started at school after the summer of 2007 in Ålesund. I wasn't there. I had to train or play a match. I know that she is angry at me because I haven't been there for her. She has every reason to be. It hurts to think about it. I'm prepared to do anything for my children but it hasn't been enough.

50

THE NATIONAL TEAM WERE PLAYING BETTER THAN IT HAD DONE IN a long time. It was great to have my brother there. The role of big brother somehow helped my game. It made me seem older and more responsible, a contrast to what I suspected the NFF thought of me. It did me good.

We had to play two qualifying matches in September 2007. The month before we had defeated Argentina at home in a friendly, where John Carew had scored both goals. First up was Moldova in Chişinău. Martin Andresen was captain, and Steffen Iversen scored the goal that secured the victory. It meant we had accrued three straight qualifying victories and scored nine goals without reply, and had climbed up to second place in the group. Awaiting us back home at Ullevaal were the group leaders, Greece.

Everything happened in the first half. We fell behind twice, the first time only seven minutes into play, but we started playing good football again. John Carew levelled after a quarter of an hour, and then, after half an hour, we were down again. But we didn't give in. We ratcheted up the pressure. I consider this match one of my best for the national team. I didn't get tired. We just couldn't lose this. This was a tournament we had to qualify for. I battled like a lunatic. And six minutes before the break I struck from twenty yards. I could tell as soon as I struck the ball that I'd made perfect contact, the way the ball easily left my foot and flew into the corner. It was a dream goal. And at 2–2 our chance of a European Championship appearance lived on. I continued to run up and down the pitch, up and down my wing, even though I could feel a groin pull, right until the referee whistled for full time.

The draw made the equation simple for us: if we won our remaining three matches, we'd qualify as group winners. The last match was against Malta, so it was the next two matches that would be decisive: Bosnia-Herzegovina away and Turkey at home one month later at Ullevaal in late November. We were only two matches from qualifying. It was all up to us. First, the Bosnians in Sarajevo. We scored after just five minutes. And we held the lead, but it was incredibly nervewracking. One little slip-up to make it 1-1 and our chances of reaching the European Championship would be microscopic. With a little less than twenty minutes remaining, I played the ball ahead to Morten Gamst Pedersen, and he swung in a cross. There – at the back of the area – my little brother comes charging in. He struck the ball well. Hard and along the ground. It went in. I could hardly believe it. I screamed in joy and ran across the entire pitch to lift him up. Over 75 yards I ran, yelling and screaming with my arms in the air.

Everything hung on the match against Turkey. We were on home ground. The match was to be played in Nordic November weather. We were so close.

51

THE STADE VÉLODROME – MARSEILLE'S HOME GROUND – IS NOT THE stadium you want to visit when only one outcome will do: victory. Otherwise, we would be out of the Champions League before the knockout stages. That would not do for a team like Liverpool. Not for a team who had been to two finals in the past three years. Especially not with the investment in players' made prior to the season. It was not even Christmas and Rafael Benítez was already in danger of getting the sack.

Marseille would advance with a draw. All the pressure was on us. When we learned the squad selection, my name was included. Maybe my place was not as threatened as the rumours in the papers would have it.

The atmosphere in the ground was menacing. The French supporters booed any time one of us touched the ball. The floodlights dazzled. But after four minutes of play they went silent as we went ahead through a penalty. And on that night – after having been all but written-off two months earlier – we were suddenly a completely different team than we had been during the autumn. We were better than Marseille in every department. When the referee blew the final whistle, the scoreboard read 4–0.

But it didn't stop the articles in the papers. Questions about my future at the club persisted. They were just rumours but I had to be on my toes, I realised that.

As a result of the speculation, Valencia contacted Liverpool. The manager Ronald Koeman believed I had the running power and an offensive style that suited his preferred 4-3-3 formation. Kevin Keegan at Newcastle was also meant to be interested. I didn't know what to believe. I wanted to give Benítez every possible reason to keep me. One bit of encouragement came from the Italian sports daily *La Gazzetta dello Sport*, which ranked me as Europe's fourth-best left-back in its annual summary for 2007: Éric Abidal (Barcelona), Philipp Lahm (Bayern Munich),

Patrice Evra (Manchester United) and then me. But in the league I continued on the bench, and it was difficult. When I started in the FA Cup against Luton, I managed to score an own goal by kicking the ball off my own left arm and into the net, making it 1-1 and leading to a replay against a team struggling in League One. I remember the photos of me, exhausted and bewildered on the grass at Kenilworth Road.

In the league we had to battle to finish among the top four and secure our qualification for the Champions League. The match against Aston Villa at the end of January was an important one. When the squad was read out, I was excluded. I was not even on the bench. That had never happened before. I was furious, but disguised it as best I could. I didn't understand a damn thing. I was fresh and free of injury. Things were good at home, all in all, everything was fine. I may have had a poor match, but so does everyone. As long as I was healthy, I was the best left-back on the team. And then there could be no doubt: I should be playing in every match.

In my fury, I thought that I had to get out of Liverpool. I was not content to be left on the bench, only to come on towards the end of matches. And now I was even left out of the squad completely. The same thing repeated itself against West Ham. I can't be fucking arsed with this, I muttered. I have to get out. I was really down at that point. Football was my job, my life, and then I was told that I couldn't be a part of it. And I couldn't understand why. But I didn't actually want to get away. I pulled myself together. I battled on. And truth be told, I was still a starter for all the big fixtures in my seventh season at Liverpool, playing against Arsenal, Chelsea, Manchester United and Everton. When I added them up at the end of the season, I had still played in 44 games, and again there were not many players with more matches: Steven Gerrard, Jamie Carragher, Pepe Reina, Dirk Kuyt, Ryan Babel and Yossi Benayoun. But I'm not going to lie. I was concerned. Something was different. I'd had Benítez's trust for several seasons, I thought he was on my side but that seemed to have changed, and that hurt.

In the first knockout round of the Champions League we faced Internazionale. In our last match before the tie', we had somehow lost 2-1 at home to Barnsley to crash out of the FA Cup with a bad taste in our mouths. Against Inter, I was benched again but we won 2-0 and Zlatan Ibrahimović, who was on the pitch for the Italians, did not contribute much more to the match than I did. We played just as well in our 1-0 victory at the San Siro in front of nearly 80,000 fans. I came on to play out the closing minutes. For the quarter-final, we drew Arsenal, and even though I had to endure a place on the bench, it was wonderful how the team responded to Arsenal levelling the tie at 2–2 in the second leg at Anfield with just six minutes remaining. At that point, we were out because we had only managed a 1–1 draw at the Emirates. But with ice in his veins, Steven Gerrard netted from the penalty spot two minutes later, and in the final minute of play, Babel added another to make it 4–2. Once again I only made an appearance at the very end.

Four teams now remained in the tournament, three of them English and one Spanish: Manchester United, Chelsea, Barcelona and us. The draw for the semi-finals put a familiar opponent in our path. We'd faced Chelsea in the semi-final both times we'd reached the final, and we were going to face them again. But unlike the previous two meetings, the first leg was going to be played at Anfield, and the second leg in London. We felt that gave us a mental edge. We had already overcome them in two Champions League semi-finals. They were good in the Premier League but as a team, we showed our best quality on the European stage. And just like the year we won the trophy, we had bounced back from a terrible start and battled on with our backs to the wall.

From virtually being knocked out during the group stage we had fought our way through to earn the chance to reach our third final in four years. It was a magnificent opportunity. For the team, obviously, but also for me. Only Chelsea stood between us and another final. I had played in both the previous encounters, and even though I was on the bench for the time being, I would have to find it in me to win back a place in the starting eleven. I was going to fight like a lion during training. I was going use my outings off the bench to prove that I deserved a place. Playing in three finals of the greatest club tournament on the planet, as well as being one of the starting eleven on all three occasions, would be an achievement that placed me in exceptionally distinguished company. I was going to fight my way back onto the team. I was going to play better than ever. I was going to get Benítez's attention. I was going to score yet another spectacular goal, and together this team was going to make history.

52

NOVEMBER AT ULLEVAAL. COLD MIST AND A CAPACITY CROWD. JOHN Carew was the first onto the pitch and I was the last. The national anthems were played. The match against Turkey started well. We got a throw-in inside their half. I threw a long ball in, Steffen Iversen flicked the ball on, and Erik 'Panzer' Hagen gave us the lead after just twelve minutes. We controlled the match. We had our fans behind us. The temperature, the weather – everything spoke to our advantage. We were in the European Championships.

After a half-hour the Turks levelled. And when we got anxious our game locked up. Fourteen minutes into the second half, they added another to make it 2–1. We failed to respond.

That night I didn't get any sleep. I had given my all but again failed when it mattered most. We were out of another championship and we had been so close this time. My little brother must have heard me crying in the bed next to him, just as I'd heard him when we were little and Dad moved out.

53

'DO YOU THINK YOU'RE AN ANNOYING PERSON?'

'Yes. I'm probably very annoying at times.'

'In what way?'

'Do you mean in real life or in the version that's been written about?'

'You choose where you want to start.'

'I realised early on that I performed best under maximum pressure. The worse the situation the better, in fact. I liked to go into a match with the sense of having a knife at my throat. Everything to avenge, everything to prove... but I don't know how consciously I created these situations, I just said things that created a lot of commotion. Like the story about Beckham's leg before my first match in England. Maybe I just enjoyed acting tough, maybe I thought that was how I had to act now that I had got to where I was. Create a bit of commotion. Anyway, the pressure that came brought out the best in me.'

'...'

'But I don't know, at some point the media started to write about me as if I actually was that person. They interpreted all the things in my life on the basis of the loud-mouthed person I pretended to be in order to succeed on the pitch. The football player and the person were mixed up and assumed to be one and the same. The journalists took it for granted that they knew who I was. Or they didn't care. They knew what sold papers. And I kind of lost control. I became the idiot who gets on everyone's nerves, even when they mentioned things unrelated to sport. It's been pretty painful for me to deal with.'

'But this guy who gets on everyone's nerves, do you think there's a bit of him in you?'

'(Laughter.) Yes. I've been involved in a few incidents that might point to that. Plenty of teammates must have thought I was too much. I've always had an *overabundance of energy and been somewhat outspoken in situations like that. It can be irritating, I get that.'*

'Where do you think that comes from?'

'I don't know. I've never had a lot of self-confidence in anything other than football. Maybe I've displayed a bit too much of it because of that. To compensate for it, somehow. I've found it difficult to find the balance. I remember fronting an anti-bullying campaign years ago. I travelled around and talked to schoolchildren about my experiences. I liked doing it. But then I was interviewed about it, and then I heard myself start to talk about the red Ferrari and how driving around in Ålesund with it was my revenge. (Laughter.) The little bit of sympathy I might have gained probably disappeared just as quickly.'

'...'

'That's not exactly been my strong point.'

54

THE FIRST LEG OF THE CHAMPIONS LEAGUE SEMI-FINAL AGAINST Chelsea was played at Anfield on 22 April 2008. Once again I was on the bench to start the match. But I was prepared, I paid attention. If the chance came, I had to seize it.

Around the hour mark at Anfield it was clear that Fábio Aurélio could not continue. I had warmed up for a while. We led 1–0 and The Kop was singing. Dirk Kuyt had managed to get the ball between the legs of Petr Čech, scoring just before the break after Frank Lampard had lost the ball on the edge of his box. We had controlled the match at home.

Benítez signalled for me to get ready. My number was given to the fourth official. He put it up on the board. Number 6. At the next whistle I was going in. I could feel the spring of the leather in the new shoes. I had prepared myself as thoroughly and precisely as always. Showered, not too cold, not too hot. Got ready. Hair gel, deodorant. Jerseys so clean they still smelled of washing powder. Brand new boots. Left sock before the right one. Then left shoe before the right. No shin guards during warm-up. Left shoe a little tighter than the right. There was a half-hour remaining. I ran out on the pitch, found my place at left-back. My first involvement went perfectly okay. I got into the match just fine. We played nice and safe at the back. With six minutes left we could have increased our lead, but Gerrard's volley flew just over, via the fingertips of Cech. But we were up 1–0, a nice result for us. If we didn't concede a goal at home, Chelsea would be in a fix in the second leg at Stamford Bridge in London. They would have to defend well while still chasing a goal. And if we got another goal down there, they would need three to keep us out of the final. Protecting the clean sheet was the most important thing now. And we had no problems. The match clock passed ninety minutes. We created a dangerous situation on a corner, with Fernando Torres forcing a good save from Čech. I took no chances, stayed back.

In the fourth minute of injury time, Salomon Kalou received the ball down in the corner on our right side. At first there seemed no danger. But he managed to swerve a cross into our penalty area. I saw the ball coming. I had to keep control of Nicolas Anelka, who was behind me, but it was my ball. I had to clear it. The ball came towards us at an awkward height. I couldn't get to it before it bounced in our six-yard area. To make sure I'd reach the ball before Anelka, I threw myself forward but had to head it on a low hop. It all happened so fast, but instead of knocking the ball out for a corner, I directed it into the top corner past a shocked Pepe Reina. The fans in The Kop stopped singing. It went completely quiet. I buried my face in the turf. God.

55

THE FIRST THING I DID WHEN I ENTERED THE DRESSING ROOM AFTER a loss was take off the bloody boots that were too small for me. I pulled the tape off my socks, rolled them down, removed my shinpads and pulled the socks off completely. My toes didn't look good. They always hurt, but never more than after a defeat. The nails were crooked and blue. I pulled off my drenched jersey and just sat there. When we lost, the body hurt all over. Nobody talked. The showers were short. We got dressed but not all spruced up like when we won. Nobody fixed their hair but just put on a cap and let it hide most of their face on the way out. When I got home, I found some comfort food. Anything I could find that was sweet and fatty, I crammed it down me.

56

THE OWN GOAL CAME WITH VIRTUALLY THE LAST KICK OF THE MATCH against Chelsea. The TV cameras followed me as I padded off the pitch. The entire world was watching. The people in the stands. People in Jakarta. The people at Miller's pub in Ålesund. I wiped my face with my strip so that nobody could see me. I looked down at my shoes, drank a little water and didn't look up. They were singing now, the fans. *You'll Never Walk Alone*. But I was so alone then. I've never felt more alone.

In the dressing room I sat with aching toes and a towel over my head. Some of the lads came over and said I shouldn't think about it. I won't say who they were. But I knew they were furious at me. Of course they were. They were disappointed and angry and had exactly the same thought I'd had when other people made blunders: you can't do that at this level. Everyone knows it happens, a tenth of a second and it's done, but that doesn't help. It's unforgivable.

They reminded me that Fábio Aurélio was injured, and that I'd be playing in the return leg.

I drove home to my house in Woolton. I ate more sweets and snacks than ever. I felt extremely sorry for myself. I always did, not just when we lost but when I was one of those to blame. I was wallowing in self-pity and chocolate.

The next day my face was plastered on every newspaper in England, and it didn't stop there. The whole world seemed to be writing about my insane own goal. My name was on everyone's lips. I didn't leave my home for days. I didn't answer the phone. I couldn't go on the internet because of all the things that were written about me. When I arrived at Melwood for a training session, I saw the graffiti on the wall: 'Riise, fuck off!!' 'Ginger, go home!' All my life I had tried to be loved.

All that was left was the own goal. It was a low point. Even the fans, that had always been on my side, that I loved, that I was willing to do just about anything for, and that I was practically dependent on, had turned against me. Those were the kind of thoughts I had. Even though it was only a handful of fans that had written that crap on the wall, it was their words that I saw. That was what I lay awake at night thinking about. And I heard this voice whirling the same sentence over and over again in my head: 'Everything is your fault, isn't it?' I know a lot of players who have struggled with that voice. Maybe it crops up with such force at times because we spend so much time blocking out all the negative thoughts. I don't know. But as soon as that voice started it wouldn't shut up. I've seen players sitting in their cars crying because they've made a huge blunder. I know that once that dam bursts, sometimes you can feel like life isn't worth living. I've tried to offer them comfort when I could. But now I was the one who needed comforting.

Eight days later we met Chelsea at Stamford Bridge. I was selected for the starting eleven. Benítez probably hoped I would once again demonstrate my ability to find my best when everything was at its worst, anyway, Fábio Aurélio's injury ruled him out of the game.

After twelve minutes Didier Drogba scored for Chelsea. Now we needed a goal. And after the break Fernando Torres finally managed to equalise with 26 minutes remaining. I worked like an animal on the rain-soaked pitch. When the referee whistled for full time, I couldn't help thinking that we should have been celebrating now. We should have been in the final again. Now we had to face extra time. Chelsea playing at home proved to be too much for us in the end. They beat us 3-2, 4-3 on aggregate.

The last thing I thought before I finally dozed off in the early hours of the morning was that I had scored the most expensive own goal of all time.

There were two matches remaining in the season, against Manchester City and Tottenham. Our place in the top four was secure. I was in the dressing room after a training session. I don't remember who, but someone poked their head in and said Benítez wanted to talk to me. There was nothing unusual about it, he used to invite players to his office for a chat. I walked down the corridor, knocked, said hello, then we sat down and he smiled at me from behind his desk. Then he said: 'I think it's time we go our separate ways. You could benefit from new challenges and we've bought a new left-back that we intend to rely on.' The last bit I had actually read about in the papers. Liverpool had purchased Andrea Dossena from Udinese for £7million, but that kind of thing had happened before. On each occasion I had accepted the challenge and emerged victorious from it. So I hadn't expected this. I just sat there, half in shock. For seven years I had played at Liverpool. Three hundred and forty-eight matches. I'd won the Champions League, the FA Cup and the League Cup.

'You're a big name, you can play anywhere at all. We'll help you find another club if you like.'

'Can I play the last two matches?' was all I could say. For some reason it was important that I reach 350 matches and an exact average of fifty per season.

Benítez just shook his head. I wanted to ask why he hadn't warned me, why he hadn't said my position was under threat so that I could have tried even harder but I said nothing. I simply declined his offer to help me find another club. After a brief silence we got up and I shook his hand. Out in the corridor I tried to collect my thoughts. I'd got the sack, plain and simple. I went back to the dressing room. Pepe Reina was there, along with Carragher and Gerrard. 'What happened?' one of them asked.

'I'm done,' I said. 'I'm done at Liverpool.'

At first they laughed because they thought I was messing about, then they went quiet. I packed my bag, zipped it up and walked out to my car, stowed it in the back like I had done so many times in all my years at the club. I opened the driver's side door and got in. I didn't start the car. I just sat there in the Melwood car park. Then I started to cry. I wondered if Maria was home, or if the house was empty. If she was out shopping, I would have to tell her when she got back. I don't know, maybe some of the calm disappeared right there in the car park outside Melwood. I loved Liverpool. I loved everything the club stood for. Now it didn't want me anymore. This pain, I couldn't just run it off. God, it really hurt.

57

I HAVE TO RESPECT RAFAEL BENÍTEZ FOR THE WAY HE DID IT. HE WAS open and honest. Straight to the point. Afterwards there was speculation as to whether it was a somewhat irrational decision made in light of the own goal against Chelsea, but that isn't right. I had simply not performed well enough throughout the season. And in the off-season I'd let myself go a bit. I can see that in hindsight. I was not a player who could afford to do that. I had to offer maximum effort at all times, work that much harder than all the others to keep my place. But the intensity sank by maybe five or ten percent. I was too comfortable in my position, and then was simply no longer good enough. And I had to pay for it. In the worst possible way.

In the car, I dried my tears. Cleared my throat. Then I rang my agent, Struan. I had one year left on my contract, and strictly speaking we'd just been waiting till the end of the season to renegotiate. Now everything was turned on its head. I could see out my final year, just train and collect my salary, but the thought of remaining at Liverpool only to sit on the bench wasn't appealing. When Benítez had said they were going to focus on Dossena, he'd also told me that a life on the bench was the best I could hope for. Even if Dossena didn't succeed, I didn't want to throw away five or six months of my career waiting around. With seven million pounds invested they were going to give him a lot of chances. I was 28 years old, and I didn't want to wait.

Marshall waited to hear what I would say.

I looked out over the car park. 'I'm done,' I said.

'What?'

'I spoke to Benítez and I'm done.'

'What the fuck?'

Then he said what agents have to say: 'Johnny. Don't worry, mate. You've had a fantastic career. Give me a few days and I'll sort this out.'

Then I rang mum and cried some more.

I didn't start the car until after I'd spoken to her. I drove out of the training facility and it was one of the hardest things I've done in my entire career. Maria and I had been together for two years. We wanted children. We'd planned to get married in the summer. How would I explain this to her? We'd have to postpone all our wedding plans now. I couldn't think about anything other than finding a new club. I had to be in top shape going forward. We'd have to move. I didn't want to play for any other club in the Premier League. My respect for Liverpool fans was too great for that. So we had to move to a new country. I remember opening the front door of the house I had lived in for seven years. 'Maria?'

58

IT HAPPENED LIKE THIS: A SUCCESSION OF AGENTS AND CLUB executives start to chat. Several clubs quickly reported their interest: Schalke, Atlético Madrid, Villarreal and Juventus. When I first found out I was going to leave Liverpool, I'd told Struan that I wanted to try something new, a different culture.

'And AS Roma,' he said. Roma had been the first to report interest in me. I have to admit, I liked the fact that they'd gone after me immediately. I'm not a game player. I don't wait and see how things play out with offers and counter-offers, that's never been my style. I was simply gushing with joy. Roma? Roma! Roma! Truth be told I'd more or less already said yes to them before the other clubs had a chance to make proper enquiries.

I spoke to Maria first, but to be brutally honest, none of it was up to her. I was a professional footballer. When a club doesn't want you any longer, it's simply a matter of moving on. For the people we live with, this is obviously a huge burden. Even though you've made your home, with loads of thought and work put into it, you still have to move when word arrives. Making plans for the future is almost hopeless. Very rarely is there time to put down roots, like I'd done at Liverpool.

'Roma? Okay,' I said. 'Make it happen.'

I was flown down. Accompanied by the police, representatives from the club met me on the plane. They escorted me through the airport so that nobody would see me. The contract was still being negotiated, and they didn't want there to be any fuss before everything was ready.

One of the club's drivers drove us into town. I opened the window and felt the heat. There were far more colours outside than in Liverpool, brighter. The landscape was practically scorched by the sun. Not damp and rainy and British. People drove scooters like they did in the movies.

We were put up in a fancy hotel, where I was told to stay in my room until Struan and the club had finished negotiating. It's a strange world, it really is. The next day I was driven to the Villa Stuart health clinic for a medical. The rumours were clearly in full swing now. Outside the gates were dozens of Roma supporters along with photographers and journalists. Then back to the hotel again, to await the results of the medical, dinner with Struan, without being able to leave the building.

On 18 June 2008, I signed a four-year contract. The transfer fee was for €5million, and I was to receive a €2.8million salary per year, which matched my salary at Liverpool. Later I was interviewed by AS Roma's own TV channel. I was to be introduced to the fans for the first time. They thought it would be a good idea to make the recording on the roof, so the first impression the Roma fans had of me was a pale, ginger man who was obviously toiling in the summer heat, bathed in sweat and struggling to understand the interviewer's broken English.

The training facility was called Trigoria and was a good distance south of the city. The players also slept there before home matches, two to a room. All the meals were eaten there. But there were no other players there when I arrived. They were still on holiday, but I was happy to train for a few days before they turned up. It was a little spooky being there alone but soon people began to arrive. And once people started arriving, there was practically no end to it. During the day the place filled up. I remember when the manager, Luciano Spalletti, went to introduce me at breakfast the day the pre-season started. There was practically no end to all the people I had to meet: doctors, physiotherapists, equipment managers, a chef, cooks and many more. They had employees for every imaginable task.

At night I watched matches from the European Championship. Italy had dropped out in the quarter-final against Spain on penalties. I saw my former teammate Fernando Torres score the winning goal in the final against Germany.

Number 6 at Roma, which had belonged to the loyal defensive giant Aldair, the Brazilian who had captained Roma, was retired, so I took number 17. It was clear that they viewed me as a big signing, and that a certain hierarchy existed, as there often does, whether articulated or not. I was not placed with the reserves but was allocated a spot at the breakfast table with Francesco Totti, Daniele De Rossi and Philippe Mexès. In the dressing room, it was the same. I was next to Mexès, who was next to Totti. I was mostly preoccupied with watching, listening and learning, just as I had been when I arrived at Liverpool, though now I had a bigger role to fill because it was expected of me. But it wasn't as easy as it had been seven years earlier. I struggled with the language. Mexès is French, so I could speak to him, Daniele De Rossi spoke English and helped me, but Italian took time to learn, and it was as though I lost a part of myself without the relaxed atmosphere. I couldn't joke around the way I wanted to. I lost my bearings a little and was afraid of coming across as thick. I lacked friends. And also, it was very, very hot. In the first league match we met Napoli in Rome. I played 73 minutes. It was August, and the sun was at its peak, the stadium was scorching and there wasn't even a puff of wind. I was so exhausted that I could barely walk off the pitch when the substitution was finally signalled.

The matches against Napoli are considered among the big clashes over the course of a season. The biggest matches for Roma supporters are obviously the derbies against Lazio, then it's Juventus, Milan and Inter, as well as Napoli. If you score against any of them, it helps in your struggle to win over the fans. Otherwise, the hearts of Roma supporters are not the easiest to win. Preferably you have to be from Rome, like Totti and De Rossi, both of them one-club men. But at the same time – what fans! Inside the dressing room you could hear the passion in their song before matches:

Roma, Roma, Roma
Core de 'sta città …
The heart of this city
The one and only love …

I get still goose pimples. Every time we came out on the pitch, the entire Curva Sud stood up and held their scarves above their heads. Immediately it started to thunder. There were enormous banners and flags that the *tifosi* had made. The matches were often late at night, so it was usually dark around the floodlights. There were songs, shouts, violent crashes and burning flares that filled the terraces with smoke. It all combined to created an almost magical atmosphere. There are few places where the football fans are more intense and emotional. They love you, and they hate you. I didn't play poorly during the autumn, but it wasn't quite working right either. I sensed that the dedicated supporters were expectant, that I wasn't living up to their high expectations. I don't know how it is for other players but for me, being accepted by the fans was crucial. I struggled without their love. And I knew that I wasn't worthy of it during the opening months. Soon it would be too late, I thought. Their patience could be in short supply. What was now scepticism could turn to opposition if I didn't improve. I lay awake at night afraid that things wouldn't turn, that things wouldn't fall into place. But all I could do was keep working hard in training sessions, in matches, making sure to squeeze the max out of my body every time. I vowed not to leave the training ground or the stadium until I was completely exhausted. Still, I had not scored a single goal for my new club.

On 1 March 2009, we met Inter. A huge clash. My thirtieth match for Roma.

At home at the Olympic Stadium they had humiliated us 4–0. Now we faced the league leaders away. We had to avenge ourselves, not least for the sake of the fans. First De Rossi gave us the lead. Then – just minutes later – I broke in from the left flank with the ball. I looked up before I shot. The ball sneaked in under Júlio César. Goal! Two-nil. I stormed towards our fans. I saw them launch themselves towards me, overcome with joy, I saw the flags waving, heard the banging and the cheering, smelled the smoke in the air. Finally.

With a 2–0 lead at the break, we were not pleased with the 3–3- result. Still, it was away against the league leaders and Inter was an impressive team with brilliant players like Luís Figo, Zlatan Ibrahimović, Adriano, Patrick Vieira, Javier Zanetti, Marco Materazzi and Hernán Crespo. And the manager? José Mourinho. He had taken over Inter before the season, and I had a tendency to score goals against his team. After the match, he came over and gave me a hug.

All things considered, Milan and the San Siro was a good place for me. In May 2009 we met AC Milan there, and once more it was as though a big match forced the very best out of me. I felt the pressure in those types of matches, but I thrived on the pressure. Around half an hour had gone when we got a free-kick about twenty yards from their goal. David Pizarro, our Chilean number 7, stood over the ball. Just like with Dietmar Hamann against Manchester United in my opening season at Liverpool, we'd arranged for Pizarro to roll the ball carefully to the left when I started my run-up. Standing in the wall were players like Massimo Ambrosini, Kaká, Filippo Inzaghi and David Beckham. I heard Dida directing them.

Pizarro judged the roll perfectly. Mathieu Flamini flew towards me and threw himself at me but I lashed the ball with my left foot. Dida was barely able to register what had happened. The ball was stuck in his left-hand corner. It was the farewell match for Paolo Maldini at the San Siro, with over 70,000 in the stands. Our fans went crazy. We led 1–0 and this was a goal that would be remembered. Milan levelled after the break but with ten minutes remaining we broke on a brilliant counter-attack. I legged it forward as usual, got the ball, nutmegging Maldini, one of my heroes. That's the way it had to be, I thought. Maybe it was bad form, in his farewell match, in front of the home fans after 25 faithful seasons at the club. But maybe not. Anyway, I'm sure one of the best left-backs of all time could live with it. What was shameful, though, was a large portion of the Milan fans booing him after the match. Unbelievable.

Jérémy Ménez got free after my subsequent pass and restored our lead. Milan levelled again, but in a dramatic conclusion to the match, with Ambrosini seeing red, Francesco Totti secured us the victory. It was one of the top matches in Serie A that season, and I was selected man of the match. I was walking on air. The amazing Roma supporters embraced me. I was one of them now, I felt. I had done it. It was the second to last league match. Things boded well for the next season, I thought. Over the course of my first season I'd played 42 matches, a record bettered only by De Rossi and Matteo Brighi. Did I miss Liverpool? I don't think I let myself. My efforts were going to be invested here at Roma. I couldn't walk around lost in a dream. We'd got a flat in a complex where all the streets in the area were named after Scandinavian cities: Via Stoccolma, Via Oslo, and the street we lived on along with Totti and De Rossi was Via Copenhagen. And Maria? My impression was that she had quickly settled in with all the luxury design shops in the Italian capital. And more importantly, she was heavily pregnant. She was due in August. The appointment for the caesarean was booked. The birth would take place in Norway before the start of the season. Soon baby sounds would fill our home again. I could hardly wait.

Matches and training sessions were hard. In the build-up to my second season at Rome I mistimed a tackle on Totti at the training ground in Trigoria, and all my weight came down on his leg. I hit him from the side, and afterwards he couldn't get up. God. I saw him writhing in pain. I was very apologetic.

He couldn't get off the pitch by himself and had to be carried off. The rest of the session was marked by what had happened. At the end of the previous season I'd finally gained the respect of the fans, then I went and did this to their favourite, a club legend. I was terrified that I had ended the captain's season before it had even begun. It wasn't until the following day that we were finally told that the injury was not as serious as first expected. I sat in the dressing room, pretended not to notice, but exhaled in relief.

The beginning of the season was chaotic. We lost the first two league matches, against Genoa and Juventus. Then manager Spalletti resigned. Claudio Ranieri was brought in. For me it was a brilliant fit. We liked each other instantaneously. I had other problems, of the sweeter sort, I suppose. Throughout the autumn of 2009 I didn't get much sleep. Emma, my second daughter, had colic, and I liked to get up and walk around with her in my arms to calm her. I pulled her blanket up over her ears to muffle the sound altogether. Maria might as well sleep. I arranged some pillows on the sofa so that I could lie down with Emma on my chest without waking her. If she started to cry again, I got up and started to walk around with her, rocking her small body, nice and gently.

We played in the Europa League against Fulham in October 2009, and my brother had just signed for them. It was huge. He played on the right side and I was on the left, so we challenged each other over and over again over the course of the two matches. And we both wore number 17 for our respective clubs. I have a picture where you can see our backs, my dark red strip and his white one, battling for the ball, both number 17s, both Riises. It was a big deal for me. I have that pic on my mobile. But let's be completely clear. If he tried to get around me, I would take him down if need be. Yes, he was my little brother and I wished him all the best, but I couldn't take that into consideration when we played a match against each other. Then there was no mercy. He would do the same to me.

We ended up in the same group. I scored in the return fixture and we pipped Fulham to win the group, though both clubs went through to the knockout stage. Hugely disappointing for us, we were knocked out immediately by Panathinaikos, while Fulham and my brother went all the way to the final, which they lost to Atlético Madrid.

In the league, however, we played quite well. All season long the battle for the title was between two teams, us and the previous year's winners, Inter. As usual I surged up and down my wing, but I was scoring and assisting more goals again now. The Italian sports papers started to use a nickname for me: Thunderbolt. And *Il gladiatore*. I was probably a little too proud of that last one, but to be called The Gladiator in Rome, that meant something extra, and it was given to me, not to De Rossi or Totti. And the nickname stuck. But I ran a lot, I really did.

In January 2010 we met Juventus in Turin having lost to them at home at the beginning of the season. Second only to Lazio, this is the match the fans are most emotionally invested in. And that is saying a lot.

Alessandro Del Piero gave the home team the lead six minutes into the second half. We couldn't afford to lose if we were to stick with Inter at the top. Midway through the half, Totti levelled from the penalty spot. But a draw wasn't good enough. We needed a victory. We had a real opportunity to take home the league title, something that had only been achieved three times in club history. The fans urged us forward with flares and bangers.

With just seven minutes remaining, I was played through by Totti, who was such a fantastic player, but the Juventus keeper, Gianluigi Buffon, came out and brought me down. He was given a red card and on his way off the pitch he gave me a high five and smiled. He's like that, impossible not to like. Despite our numerical advantage, the match was poised to end in a draw. But then David Pizarro won the ball in the middle. He made his way up the right side before knocking in a cross in front of goal. This was in the dying moments of injury time. God knows what I was doing inside the box so late in the match, but thereI was at the far post, and there was the ball, and I headed it past their second-choice keeper, Alex Manninger, and then all hell broke loose. I plunged towards our fans in the corner, and my teammates came thundering towards me like a freight train, threw themselves on top of me, before we jumped over the advertising hoarding and celebrated with the fans. The photographers flocked around us. Later, in the dressing room I was told that Sky Sports Italia wanted to interview me. And I was so exhilarated, proud as a peacock I said yes. Then the person added: 'In Italian.'

The language still wasn't there. As a father with young children, I didn't have much time to practise. And I stood in the showers. I showered and showered and hoped that the programme's broadcast time might finish before I emerged. But no. They were waiting. This was a TV broadcast with a pretty big studio audience. They have a panel. And a host. In front of all these people I had to speak on a big screen. I shut my eyes for a moment. A producer asked: 'Are you there?'

'Yes.' Dripping with sweat and now this.

'Then we're live.'

And then I was on. The host asked me something I barely understood, so I just thanked her for inviting me onto the programme because I could say that. She laughed and suddenly something clicked. I just launched into it. Not grammatically correct, obviously, but I didn't care. I chatted away. I was no longer nervous. I'd scored this goal, and there I was on the big screen going on in something resembling Italian. I apologised for my Italian when I was done, but the studio audience just applauded. The fans liked that I had respected them by speaking Italian, and I think they also liked that I didn't seem to worry too much about putting my foot in it on TV. I felt like I was fully welcomed into the fold after that.

The league wasn't decided until the last week of the season. We won our final match, but it didn't matter because Inter did the same, and in the end we had to settle for second place, just two points behind the winners. It was rough, once again I had lost a league title right on the finishing line. Roma had plenty of second-place finishes. It didn't help our mood that we also lost against Inter in the cup final. The fact that I had played more matches than anyone on the team over the course of the season was of little comfort.

Even though I didn't let myself spend too much time thinking about Liverpool, and even though I felt I'd been accepted by fans and teammates, there was something I was missing at Roma. The language was definitely a barrier. I had two years remaining on my contract but few people I could speak to. In Liverpool this happened automatically, I could chat with everyone, Bernie who drove the taxi, Smally on the massage table, teammates, the man with the watches, fans who stopped me in the street, people in the shops. Here there was only Maria and me. We were getting on each other's nerves, tired parents who spent way too much time together.

I rang Nikola.

His wife was a physiotherapist; they'd met at Melwood. I wonder if they wanted to move to Rome. I could use his friendship, and I could hire his wife as my personal physiotherapist. I hoped to extend my career, I was 29, and what could be better than to have him there and her looking after my aches and pains, taking charge of massage and treatment for minor injuries that cropped up? I would offer her a salary that they both could live on, and I would pay for their flat. Maybe I was trying to recreate the positive atmosphere from the one and a half years he lived with me in Liverpool? 'What do you think?'

I was so happy when he said yes. Even happier when I saw him arrive with Amanda, with all their moving boxes in the car. It was like reliving the memory of when he arrived with his family and moved into our street on Slinningsodden when we were both children. The only thing missing was me standing there doing keepy-ups. I waited outside their flat to help with the lifting. They were going to live practically next door to us. I'd really missed Nikola.

I rarely struggled with injuries but it had been a long time since I'd played a match without it hurting somewhere, so there was plenty to do for my new physiotherapist. At the same time I loved to push my limits. At a training session the day before a league match against Udinese in November 2010, I injured my knee. I was carried off the training pitch on a stretcher. The doctors were worried. They thought it could take as many as eight or nine weeks before I could even think of training again. After three weeks I asked the doctors if it would worsen the injury if I played. No, they said, but it would be incredibly painful. That was fine by me. Pain I could deal with. I liked that it cracked, that it hurt. Against Milan I was back. We won 1–0. And one of those days – whether it was right before or right after the Milan match, I don't remember – I made a Norwegian in Rome happier than I ever remember seeing anyone before. The former politician Anders Hornslien lived in Rome and had become a big Roma fan. He was turning forty. I didn't know him but some of his friends asked if I could get a match jersey from Totti, signed and sweated in. It was no big deal. I asked Francesco and he gave me the one he'd worn for the final match of the group stages of the Champions League on the Wednesday. I've never seen anyone as happy as Anders Hornslien that night. It was so contagious that I stayed at his party for several hours.

Years later, I watched Francesco's farewell match from afar and the tribute to him after 25 seasons and 786 matches at the same club. I couldn't keep it together, especially when his children came on the pitch. I sat in my living room sobbing. Louise came in wondering what in the world had happened. But I was just really touched. I cry a lot but, I mean, this was really beautiful.

59

WERE MARIA AND I HAPPY? YES, FOR A WHILE I SUPPOSE WE WERE. We had Emma after three years. She went to an Italian nursery, where I dropped her off and picked her up. Apart from that, the majority of everyday tasks fell to Maria, as it does for anyone who lives with an elite athlete. We bickered a lot. It wasn't just her. Things were different when we left Liverpool. Even with Nikola and his wife living in Rome we were isolated. I was happy, Roma was a fantastic club, but I'd spent seven seasons at Liverpool. I had lived there for seven years. The house in Woolton had been my home for a long time. I'd been through a marriage and a divorce there. Ariana had learned to walk in that house. I had lived there with Nikola and we'd been inseparable at the time, both single; in Rome we had our families to take care of. It might never be the same in Rome. I didn't have that many years left as a player. I was at another place in my career. There would not be seven years here. No, I did not have the same calm, a restlessness might have sneaked in when I started to see the end of my career. I wanted to experience as much as possible. As a football player I could move almost anywhere. I no longer had unlimited time remaining.

I looked at Maria. I remember thinking that my life would be happier without her but she was Emma's mum, and I didn't want to be somebody who simply gave up. I wanted to be loyal. In certain situations I find it incredibly hard to say things that I know will hurt people. It must be a fear, maybe a fear of me being abandoned, I don't know. Instead I wait. Wait and wait. Right up until it's impossible to wait any longer.

The summer of 2010 – the year after Emma was born – we got married. I'm embarrassed to say it because I can see in hindsight that I did exactly the same thing in two relationships: I proposed because eventually it felt like the last resort.

Twice I got married even though I knew it wasn't right – even before the ceremony. I don't know if I can explain how that could happen. But it happened. I hadn't learned a thing. And I have to admit, when I look back on various events in my life, there's one question that often comes back to me: have you really learned anything?

I want to be someone who learns from his mistakes, who grows and develops because of these experiences. I don't know why it's so difficult for me. But I don't give up. In the end I'll get things right.

I wanted to keep a lower profile than last time. We invited 35 guests to come to New York with us. Mum and Thormod were there. My brother and his wife. Nikola. Ariana was there. She was nine then, so incredibly pretty in her dress. The party was held at the top of a hotel that had a balcony going round the entire skyscraper and that offered a 360-degree view of the city. I remember how during the wedding ceremony, Emma was pulled up to the front in a little cart. She was carrying the rings on a small pillow. We were happy that night.

60

FOOTBALL PRESIDENTS ARE A BREED APART. AFTER INTERNATIONAL matches they always feel the need to stand up and say something over dinner. Never prepared. Always after hours of drinking. Teeth and lips stained with red wine, slurred speech. As players we viewed their appearance as the high point of the night when it came to entertainment. The one most disliked by the players during my time was without a doubt Norway's Yngve Hallén. After he was voted in, I remember how he didn't take the trouble to attend Norway's first international of his tenure, when we faced Ukraine at Ullevaal, where we faced Ukraine. It was disrespectful. When questioned by a journalist I spoke my mind – I thought it was disappointing for a new president. This was in 2010, and I had played 87 matches. At the next international meet-up, after the summer, Hallén approached me and took me to one side.

'We deal with these things internally,' he said. 'It makes me look bad.'

Hallén got up to all sorts of things. There was one thing he obviously thought was hilarious. Whenever one of us scored, he would give us a hundred-kroner note (worth just under £10) out of his own pocket. He would have a good laugh about it. After every dinner he would get up and dole them out. I'll never forget it. How he'd stick his hand in his pocket and ask John Carew to come up because he'd scored a goal.

61

THE UEFA CUP MATCHES AGAINST FULHAM AND BJØRNI IN THE autumn of 2009 had planted a thought in me, without me being aware of it. One and a half years later I was in no doubt: I wanted to play with my brother. He was struggling to get playing time at Fulham and I hoped I could be a support for him. The club had also done quite well in recent seasons. In 2010 they played in the UEFA Cup final against Atlético Madrid after having knocked out clubs like Juventus and Hamburg. The matches against Juventus were particularly memorable. They lost 3–1 in Turin but managed to turn it all around at home, scoring four goals at Craven Cottage. I also had some notion of completing the circle – Fulham was the club I was originally meant to join when I was headed to the Premier League from Monaco in 2001. It was the contract with Fulham that I had as good as signed at Jean Tigana's vineyard. That felt like ages ago. It was.

I had one year left on my contract with Roma and the club were already interested in extending it by another year. They pressed, but I wasn't sure. Rumours spread remarkably quickly in the football world. As soon as there was chatter that I was thinking of leaving Roma, clubs started to make enquiries. One of them was Lazio, Roma's arch-rivals. Struan informed me of the interest from the other Rome club. I didn't need to think about it, I wasn't going there.

Things were not going well with Maria. But then she was pregnant again. That was in March 2011. Maybe a change would be good for us; returning to England might save our marriage.

Maria liked the idea of living in London, and I liked the idea of a return to the British climate. And, I could see my brother every day.

In the spring of 2011 I rang Struan and told him to limit his search to England, and I mentioned Fulham specifically. Martin Jol was their new manager and he liked me,

I knew that. I asked Bjørni to find out if he might be interested, while Struan spoke to the club directors. Fulham is a nice club. What attracted me was that it was smaller, more like a family, and Craven Cottage is a lovely intimate stadium. They had a good team, too: Bobby Zamora, Damien Duff, Danny Murphy, Clint Dempsey, all good people. At the same time I saw my career slowly drawing to a close and with that in mind, Fulham could be a good club to be part of. I was turning 31 years old.

In July 2011, I signed a three-year-contract with Fulham. After three years at Roma, Maria, Emma and I packed our things. Emma hadn't turned two yet. We gave most of our household furniture away to family and friends. As a footballer, it gets to the point where you can get used to only taking the most important belongings from one place to the next. It was the same when Guri, Ariana and I left Monaco. It's mainly the belongings with important sentimental value that you keep with you. For me there's just one thing: the photo album with photos of my dad and me. I've brought that with me everywhere. Now I was packing it away again. I'd done better than most. Just three clubs in thirteen seasons. And anyway, everyone in the game knows what it's about. Professional footballers often have to move house at short notice, selling and leaving places and people that they have grown to love. Whether it's the pub landlord who always shouted 'goal!' when I passed him in the street, or the butcher on the corner who I used to have a chat with. There are a plenty of people I find myself missing. Smally and Bernie from my time in Liverpool, Tim Cahill, but also my closest friends. Like Nikola. Twenty years ago he was my salvation in many ways, when he arrived with his family and intruded into my loneliness. Nikola had been with me the whole way but when Maria and I moved to London, he and his wife remained in Rome. They're still married, have two children. They live in a terraced house in the Norwegian city of Sandnes. I know that much. But that's all I know about him now.

When Maria and I arrived in London with our things, we'd been married for one year. Patrick was going to be born on 19 November. As with my other children, we knew the exact day. They have all been delivered by caesarean section. It was the only way I could make sure I was there. Obviously I could have missed a home match, but what if I was away, what if I didn't make it back? I had to be there for the births. There are so many things we miss out on, Christmases and birthdays and all that, so this was important. All three of my children were born by caesarean. All three of them are amazing. It's not their fault that things turned out the way they did.

At ten past nine on the morning of our chosen Saturday, Patrick was born in London. I had one last desperate thought, that this lovely, tiny little thing might make everything better for us.

62

FROM THE OUTSET, A CRUCIAL SOURCE OF MOTIVATION HAS BEEN TO prove that people were wrong about me. I amounted to much more than what everyone said. I've always been bursting with a desire for revenge, a ferocious desire to get even and disprove everything. This personality trait has been a huge advantage for me in the pursuit of achieving maximum performance as a professional footballer. But where does it come from? That's probably a question most people ask when they grow up – why am I the way I am?

I was just born combative, maybe it's as simple as that. At the same time, I don't quite believe that. There are certainly individual events that have marked me, the same goes for everyone. Pointing them out is difficult, but it's clear that my sense of loneliness growing up left its mark. The experience of not being liked by the other children must have had a similar impact. Or the fact that my dad, even though I have an extra one, died at the age of nearly 41. The fact that we didn't speak together in the final years, that as a child I wondered whether he didn't love me because I didn't hear from him. These things must mean something.

I'm older now. I can see certain things from more clearly from a distance. Why do I remember leaving Jean Tigana's vineyard without saying goodbye, even though I was twenty when it happened? Why does it still make me feel me stupid? I suppose because I've been more scared of what people would think about me than I've been willing to admit. I've always had a strong desire to be liked, and when we're talking about football fans, I've wanted them to love me. I've been willing to do just about anything for them, just like with my friends and my family. A good friend or ally should be willing to go a long way. Friends should stand by your side when things are tough. I've tried to do that with those I believed were my friends.

So who knows, maybe the desire to be liked has been just as strong as the vengefulness? Maybe those two things are simply inextricably linked?

When I arrived at Liverpool, for example. In many ways my happiness was two-fold. On the one hand, the people who'd said I was worthless had been proven wrong. On the other hand, they couldn't help but like me now. But it wasn't always that simple. Despite my success, there have still been times over the years where I have sat down on the edge of my bed yearning for people to like me.

I've tried to remind myself that nobody can be liked by everyone, that's just the way it is. I've told myself that probably ninety percent of people like me. But the way I'm built, I haven't been able to think about anything other than the ten percent who don't. Why don't they like me? What am I doing wrong?

I've done my best to be reasonable and rational. I know it's impossible to be liked by everyone. But I couldn't stop trying. Something deep inside me wasn't able to let go. I see that now.

63

IN LONDON I SLEPT IN THE GUEST ROOM WITH PATRICK. HE WAS ONLY two months old and I was the one to get up with him during the night. I loved walking around with him, just like I had enjoyed walking around with Emma when she was a baby and we lived in Rome.

But I knew it couldn't continue like this. We were not doing well. We argued all the time. Nobody was doing well the way things were. The children were little, Patrick just a baby, Emma two and a half, but I couldn't stand being at home. I got up and packed two bags. Then I went into the kitchen where Maria had her back to me, cooking.

'I think we should get a divorce,' I said.

She calmly turned towards me. 'Okay' she said.

Then she turned back to the cooker.

64

MY THREE YEARS AT FULHAM WERE BY NO MEANS WHAT I HAD expected. I was given a fairly free role at left-back but never scored. Not one goal. It still bothers me. I got divorced for the second time. I only saw the children I loved sporadically. I had taken the initiative in both divorces, but I was lonely and depressed. I mean, a twice-divorced father of three, 31 years old. I lived with my brother and his wife. I'd decided to get sterilised. I was just going to wait till the end of the season, then have the procedure in the summer. The whole thing was rather distressing. I didn't tell anyone – as usual I barely spoke to other people about how I felt – but it was a time where I considered just giving up and running away from everything. I wanted to disappear off the face of the earth. I didn't want to die, that wasn't it. But I didn't want to be there with everyone else.

In February 2012 there was an international break. I travelled to Belfast to play a friendly against Northern Ireland. There was a lot of talk about how I was closing in on the record for most matches played in Norwegian colours. The match in Belfast would be number 101 and with that I would pass Henning Berg, who was number two on the list. The reporters wanted to know how it felt, that in all probability I would surpass Thorbjørn Svenssen's record of 104 caps that year. To be the player with the most matches for the men's national team ever, that was a tick on my way to achieving the goal I had set myself as a thirteen-year-old. But I didn't think about that now. I was miserable. I was happy to be out of my marriage, but miserable that I was divorced. I thought about the kids. I'd get so worried that they would be affected by it, I still do. Like all parents I cross my fingers and hope I haven't hurt my children too much. Because I haven't always been there for them. I really haven't. And it's incredibly painful to think about. Have I been just like my father? I'll look at the photo of the two of us I have on my mobile. He's playing with me, I'm very little, and the first thing I notice is how alike we are. Have I – without intending to – been the same kind of father he was?

I've tried to shut out the thoughts by keeping myself busy with other things. I sat in the hotel room trying to set up a Facebook profile. I started to add people, and suggestions kept popping up for other people I might know. Amidst this stream of profiles a picture of a woman turned up, and I thought she was insanely beautiful. I kept sitting there staring at it. I went on her profile and saw that she had registered herself as single. I sent her a friend request, but I convinced myself that she wouldn't accept it. I didn't know her, and everything she knew about me she'd got from the media. That guy. And anyway, my looks hardly helped. My confidence in my looks was no better than when I was back at the playground. Still isn't, really. Pale and ginger.

But then – only five minutes later – I was informed that Louise Angelica Markussen had accepted my request, and that we were now friends on Facebook. Hello? She really was the most beautiful woman I'd seen. I decided to DM her and see what I could come up with. For forty minutes I sat writing, deleting, writing and deleting. In the end I shut my eyes and pressed send. I wrote that she didn't have to reply, I would understand if she didn't, but what if, I mean, in case, against all expectation, maybe we could meet straight away? I regretted it at once. Minutes passed. No reply. What a dolt I'd been. I walked around the room. Checked my phone. Kept walking around. I went on like this for an hour. Checked the phone, wandered to and fro, checked again, swore at myself, checked, shook my head, but then suddenly I saw a reply. I couldn't believe it.

'Hi,' it read. That alone was beautiful, I thought. A little hello. She wrote 'hi' to me. 'I'm at work. So I didn't see your message till now.' Of course, I thought. She was at work. People are working. That's why. And here I'd been beside myself with despair and regret. 'Such a lovely message,' she wrote. 'Thanks.'

That's all there was, but I was over the moon. She chose not to respond to my request to meet straight away, but I understood that. I shouldn't have asked that. I should have waited. What kind of idiot asks that right away?

The only problem now was that I had to come up with an answer. And quick, I thought. Quick, quick, quick. While she's still there. Write something! Anything.

One word at a time. 'Hi!' Good. Then one more. 'You replied!' I wrote. No, no, no. That's pathetic. Delete. I looked at the screen. 'Hi!' was all that was left. Come on now, lad! Keep it simple, stupid. Keep it simple. 'Where do you work?' was my faltering reply in the end.

'Now, I work at a clothes shop in Lørenskog, a suburb of Oslo.'

Soon we were pinging messages back and forth on Facebook. She lived in Høybråten in Oslo, up near Stovner. She was 21 and I was ten years older than her. I didn't think much about it, I must admit. Anyway, she was probably more grown-up than I was, strictly speaking. For weeks I tried to put my very best self forward as we messaged each other. In the end she gave in to my persistence. I had to go to Oslo to take care of a few things, but she suggested we steer clear of the city centre to avoid being spotted. My brother and I had to return to London and she said she could meet us in Lillestrøm, one of the stops on the airport express train. Lunch at the Big Horn Steak House. Maybe not the most romantic place in the world, but that was where we first met. And my brother was there. I was so scared of being late that I got there more than half an hour early. I didn't say anything when my brother tried to talk to me. I just stared at the door and wiped my hands on my trousers. God, she actually came!

My brother made his excuses, he had some errands to sort out, and then we were alone. I can't remember a word of what was said.

I was in complete ecstasy afterwards. I was mincing about the station in Lillestrøm. It nearly got to the point where I had to sprint back and forth, like during training, to release the energy. I picked up my mobile again. I couldn't wait any longer. Playing hard to get has never been my strength. Come to London, I wrote. I suggested that she bring some friends with her, so she didn't think I was a creep. I didn't want her to feel uncomfortable. *But come to London.*

In London we decided to be a couple.

I remember the first time I was at her place. She lived with her mum in a terraced house. It was the first time I spent the night there. The house was empty when we got home at night. Her mum wasn't home. Louise had a room in the basement. And I remember waking up. I was thirsty, I think. And I shuffled up the stairs. I was only wearing boxers. And there – standing in the kitchen – was her mum, oh boy.

'Hi,' I ventured. 'Uh, Louise is downstairs.'

'I hope so,' she said.

That's how I met my mother-in-law for the first time. Later we had breakfast together, all three of us.

I didn't know Louise that well yet, but I felt it straight away. There was something special about her. For one thing, she wanted to come to my matches, she was curious about what I did for a living, and she kept asking me to say how I felt. We were allies from the start. That's what it felt like to me. If I stood by her side, then she would stand by mine. In everything that happened in my life, she would not waver. It was the greatest declaration of love I've ever experienced. She was my salvation.

I knew that I loved her, I knew that she was 21, and she'd said that she wanted children at some point in the future. I cancelled my appointment at the sterilisation clinic.

65

I SAT ON THE BED OF A HOTEL ROOM IN REYKJAVÍK. I SHOULD REALLY have been in a festive mood. The following day we were to open our qualification campaign for the World Cup in Brazil. It was going to be my 105th match for the national team. After that I would finally be enthroned at the top of the list of men's national-team players. I would break Thorbjørn Svenssen's record from 1962. He was 38 when he set it, I was still 31. I had more matches in me, so I wasn't just going to break this record that had been considered virtually unbreakable, in all probability I was going to end up beating it by a good margin.

In advance of the match against Iceland I'd received a call from the NFF. They called to ask if I wanted some kind of gift when the record was broken. At first I was a little surprised. Not at any point in my career did I get the sense that they actually wanted me on the national team. Whenever I was the centre of some media storm, they were the first to distance themselves from me. Now they wanted to do something for me. I was pretty chuffed. I tried to think of something that would show their appreciation, maybe a framed photo of various occasions with the national team, short anecdotes from the lads I'd played with, something like that. But then I thought back to the time my friends had taken me to Peppes Pizza the night before I left for Monaco, something personal and genuine.

'What would you like, then?' the person from the association asked.

'I'd really appreciate a dinner with the lads I've played with,' I replied.

66

THE MATCH AGAINST ICELAND WAS A DISASTROUS OPENING TO OUR World Cup qualification campaign. We started positively, but all the air was knocked out of us when Iceland scored after a long throw-in after only twenty minutes. With nine minutes remaining, we were caught out trying to play offside and they increased their lead to 2–0.

At the banquet afterwards I received a painting.

Four days later we would play at home against Slovenia. It was virtually a must-win. I remember Louise drove in and picked me up at Hotel Bristol, where the team was staying. She drove us out to Frogner Park. We parked around the back. For hours we walked among the statues. We talked about all kinds of things. She made me laugh and got my mind off things. We sat down by the Monolith, just sat there for a while, and I held her hand.

Slovenia took the lead after seventeen minutes. But we didn't lose heart. I played well. Luckily we managed to level just ten minutes later. Markus Henriksen was able to nod in a rebound off the crossbar into an open net. But then we pressed and we pressed, without creating very much. I fought like a lion. We needed another goal. Then – three minutes into injury time – Alexander Søderlund was brought down and the referee whistled for a penalty. I could hear the cheers from the terraces but then everything went quiet in my head. Moa Abdellaoue was our regular penalty-taker, but he had been substituted. The same went for number two on the list, Tarik Elyounoussi. Espen Ruud was due to take the penalty. I don't know if he got nervous or what, because it was an incredibly important kick. If he missed, Norway's chances of reaching the World Cup would be finished. After the match our manager Egil Olsen compared it to the penalty Kjetil Rekdal took against Brazil in

Marseille in the 1998 World Cup. Espen Ruud didn't step forward. I was the fourth choice penalty-taker. It was my match, it was my opportunity.

I walked with my eyes fixed on the bench and pointed at myself. I so wanted to take this penalty kick. After everything that had happened, I wanted to take the ball, put it down quietly on the penalty spot and calmly line it up. I knew I could miss. Everyone can miss a penalty. But I also knew that I could endure the storm that would await me. Probably better than any of the other designated penalty takers. I had experience. I had won.

The assistant coach Ola By Rise pointed back at me and gave me the thumbs up.

Then there was no sound. I looked at the ball. The opposing players tried to put me off by getting in my way and disturbing me and as though in a dream, I saw my brother pushing them away. For a moment – like in the Champions League final in Istanbul – I thought about doing a Panenka. It would have been fun. But no – I was going for full power. Because that's me. That's my left foot. It was the third minute of injury time. Just me and their poor keeper … complete silence. A number of players turned away because they didn't dare to look. Louise was sitting in the stands. Mum. This is my moment, I thought. Then I ran towards the ball.

The penalty against Slovenia was my sixteenth goal in 106 internationals. The next day Jan Åge Fjørtoft told me that statistic was unparalleled in international football for a defender. He had thought Brazil's Robert Carlos might have comparable figures but the Real Madrid left-back had stopped at eleven goals.

I got two hours of sleep that night. I was in Hollywood. I got this feeling, maybe now I'd done it? Was I now the best Norwegian footballer ever?

67

I PLAYED MY 110TH AND FINAL MATCH FOR NORWAY IN A 1–0 LOSS to Albania. It was not the finale I had imagined, but that match at Ullevaal on 22 March 2013 saw the end of my international career.

On 6 May 2013 I issued a press release saying that I was retiring from the national team with immediate effect. I wrote that I wanted to concentrate on club football at Fulham. I was 32 and I planned to play four or five more years of top-tier football. I had reached an age where I had to choose my priorities.

It was sad. I'd always loved playing for Norway, and I put all my heart into it. Playing for the national team was my boyhood dream.

When I walked off the pitch at Ullevaal for the last time with the Norwegian flag on my chest, with my feet aching, I was unbelievably proud. All the same, those were difficult steps.

Egil Olsen, the manager of the national team, sent me a text message a little later: 'Thanks for everything'. It was the only one I received from official quarters. I never heard any more from the NFF about the dinner.

68

IN MY FINAL SEASON AT FULHAM I WAS LEFT OUT OF THE TEAM FOR most of the autumn. I started the second and third league fixtures but then, for the next match – against West Bromwich Albion – I was not even on the bench. My name was again missing against Chelsea. Again against Cardiff City, Stoke City, Crystal Palace, Southampton. Not even on the bench. Nearly a hundred days would pass before I started again for Fulham. I never received any explanation as to why. I had good training sessions, I was in tip-top shape. I hadn't had any rows with Martin Jol or anything like that, yet all the same he had suddenly and inexplicably frozen me out. At one point I'd suggested staying at home to train instead of travelling to an away match that I wasn't going to play anyway, but I don't think that was the reason. Maybe he just preferred Kieran Richardson to me, if so, that's the manager's right. Anyway, it certainly wasn't due to the famous saying 'never change a winning team', because we didn't win many matches.

After losing 3–0 to West Ham on the last day of November, we met up to do some light training on the Sunday. We waited for Martin Jol out on the pitch at our training facility, Motspur Park near Kingston upon Thames. Someone had spotted the club's administrative director at the facility in the morning, which was unusual for a Sunday morning, and when the coach René Meulensteen arrived alone, we started to form our own opinions. When Martin Jol didn't show up for the training at all, we realised that he'd been sacked. It was all over for Jol, and playing against Tottenham three days later, I was back in the squad. And in the starting eleven. But we were in big trouble. We continued to lose. Sometimes in embarrassing fashion – 6-0 at Hull City, 4-1 at home against Sunderland. We were in imminent danger of being relegated. But we seemed to be able to elevate ourselves against the top teams. At Old Trafford we managed a draw against Manchester United. And in the next match, Liverpool awaited us. For me it was odd every time we played against them, strangest when we visited Anfield and I sat in the away dressing room. But that's professional football, and this time the match was to be played at Craven Cottage. Again we seemed to perform better against one of the big teams. We led 1–0 and 2–1 but ended up losing. After the match we were told to take four days off, to think of anything other than football. The league had a ten-day break. Then there were twelve matches remaining. We could still manage it if we pulled ourselves together. I went to back to Norway with Louise. We were going to celebrate our engagement. I'd proposed on Christmas Eve.

Other players booked flights, took their wives and children and left. Everyone was looking forward to some family time, something there's not usually much of. And particularly now when all the adversity had meant that most of us were pretty grumpy and difficult at home. We needed a little free time, to give us and our families a little breathing space.

The day after Louise and I arrived and checked into a lovely room at the Radisson Blu, with a view of the slopes and the snow, my phone beeped. We were in bed, about to sleep. It was a text from the club. René Meulensteen had been sacked. Felix Magath, the German coach, was hired to replace him. He demanded that we report for training the next day. No matter where we were.

Felix Magath is without a doubt the worst manager I've had. The first thing he said when we met him was: 'I'm sure you've heard a lot about me. For good and for bad. None of it is true.'

The truth was that we had not heard much about him. Anyway we barely understood what he said because his English was so bad. This was his first time managing a team outside Germany, and there were few indications that he'd ever had to speak anything other than German.

With Brede Hangeland struggling with a thigh injury that wasn't healing quickly enough, Magath called him into his office. 'You have to put cheese on it,' he said.

'Cheese?'

Magath wanted Hangeland to buy quark, a cheese spread that is popular in Germany, to treat his injury.

'Rub it on the thigh?'

'You can buy it at Tesco. We can send the doctor.'

Brede came down to the gym later and told us about it. I remember there were doctors and physiotherapists there. They nearly laughed themselves to death. The players' trust in Magath wore thin very quickly. And the club doctor quit not long afterwards.

We started to wonder if he was simply a little deranged. Eventually we realised that this was his method, to try and break us down mentally and physically.

For me everything came to a head when I asked for time off to marry Louise. The season had just finished in relegation. We were meant to have a summer holiday. But Magath suddenly demanded that we stay behind and train for two weeks. He thought our break would be too long, otherwise. The problem was that we had planned the wedding on the basis that I would get four weeks off, like everyone did. We had booked the church and the party in Oslo, and then a honeymoon to the Maldives and Dubai, before she joined me in Brazil for the World Cup where I was working in the media, and finally to Las Vegas. For weeks she had been surfing the net to find out everything Khloe Kardashian normally did in Los Angeles, and where. Where she shopped, where she ate, where she went out, where she lived.

So I knocked on the door of Magath's office and explained the dilemma I now found myself in. He was a small guy, with a face that looked a little like a garden gnome.

From then on it was fairly clear that I didn't have much of a future under his management. I was out of contract, which only had a few weeks remaining. Louise and I got married on the most beautiful day in May that Oslo had ever seen. The church bells rang, and Ariana carried in the rings. The tears were flowing, mine, of course. I was happy.

But this was not exactly an ideal way to prepare for a new club, that much is clear. I was without a club for the entire summer. In the autumn I was going to turn 34. In truth I considered giving up. But then, barely a month before my birthday, I finally signed a two-year contract with the champions of Cyprus, APOEL Nicosia. Not an obvious choice, but APOEL was the only one that was going to play in the Champions League. Cyprus, why not? The Mediterranean and the Champions League at the same time. Orange trees right outside the house and olive groves on the property.

The fact that it was Cyprus, a little off the beaten track, kind of felt nice. I was starting to get worn down.

A few days later, in September 2014, Felix Magath was sacked by Fulham. He was in charge of the team for twenty matches. There were only four victories.

69

THIS SHOULD HAVE BEEN A NICE STORY. ON ONE OF OUR FIRST DAYS in Las Vegas we hired a car, drove four hours to Los Angeles with Louise acting as navigator, and went to the addresses she had found. She's a bit mad when it comes to Khloe Kardashian but I can't help but think it's sweet. We stopped outside Villa Restaurant in Woodland Hills, Health Nut in Calabasas, Nobu in Malibu. We went to the design district in West Hollywood, and we drove to Hidden Hills and stood outside the gates to see if she would decide to emerge from her home. Two proper stalkers. We were having a great time and acting like the diehard fans we are, or at least Louise is.

In Las Vegas we caught wind of a rumour that Khloe Kardashian was going to celebrate her birthday at an exclusive nightclub called Tao. We were on a roll, so why not, we thought. Let's just keep going. On top of everything, we managed to get a table at the club for our guests and us. There were around sixteen of us.

I kept an eye on the entrance, maybe because Louise's lunacy was rubbing off on me, but more likely out of sheer love and a desire to make my wife happy. Suddenly a big entourage appeared by the door and in the midst of it all I spotted Khloe Kardashian. I bent over to Louise and – trying not to squeal – whispered: 'There she is! There she is! There! Look!'

As I said, we were on a roll in Vegas, so naturally it turned out that we were at a table close to theirs. After a while I got up and, trying to be as natural as possible, approached one of her bodyguards. I explained that we were just married and my wife was one of Khloe Kardashian's biggest fans, was it possible for a quick chat? That would be my ultimate wedding present for Louise.

He shook his head. Then said he: 'But you can always send a bottle of wine to the table, then we can see what happens?' I was geared up now and immediately ordered a bottle of champagne, it was her birthday, after all. What else was I going to order, was I going to choose a particular bottle of red or white wine, the guy who never drinks and doesn't know a single winemaker? No, it had to be a bottle of champagne. 'Send it to Miss Kardashian,' I said, then I waited. When I saw the waiter going over with our bottle, I watched her closely, and when she looked to where the waiter pointed, I smiled. She mouthed a thank you in the loud music. Snoop Dog was DJing, and in return I signalled if it was okay to get a picture. She nodded.

'Come on, Louise! Come on! She said yes!'

I took a picture of us with my mobile. Louise took one with hers. We got both a kiss on the cheek. Louise was in seventh heaven. And we each posted our pictures on Instagram. Who wouldn't?

It was late when the bill arrived. I hadn't seen the price when I ordered, maybe it didn't say. It was that kind of place. You didn't ask, either. Anyway, I was barely able to hear myself think in there. So I was a little shocked, I have to admit. Four thousand dollars. In my head I converted that into Norwegian currency. Thirty thousand kroner. Yeah, exactly. But I was happy to pay, it was my gift to Louise.

The story should have stopped there. But it didn't take long before one of the online papers called me. Someone had tipped them off. That happens a lot. I shouldn't care about it but I do. Soon, there was a story on the net saying I had paid thousands for a selfie with Khloe Kardashian. A romantic gesture reduced to something cheap. And what bothered me most was that someone from our group must have been the anonymous source in the matter. How else did the reporter know how much the champagne cost? That person must have been one of our friends at the table. I don't know who but it was one of those sixteen. It's hard to believe. It means I still don't have the friends I think I have. That's how I see it. And I'm probably overreacting, I know. I think my experience as a bullying victim means that I get exceedingly happy with people who want to be my friend. I start off my friendships by giving my all but then a fear creeps in that I'm being naive. Do they just want me to pay for them? It's like I'm just walking around waiting to be betrayed. Maybe I'm imagining things.

I try my best to grow. I want to be a better person. I don't want to judge people. It's not a case of you're either for me or against me, even though I'm quick to feel that way. I have to stop acting like a classic bullying victim. It's not me against the world.

I don't need to walk in the darkness to draw strength from it any longer. I don't need to boast so that people know that I'm something. I don't need to peddle my success to show that I've made it. I am someone.

70

ONCE MY INTERNATIONAL CAREER CAME TO AN END IN MAY 2013, I chose to enter a sponsorship agreement with Betsson. A key part of that decision was that it would give me an opportunity to play poker. There's a lot about poker that fascinates me, but part of what appealed to me the most was the motley crew of participants you came across. These were people who didn't fit in, I imagined. I was one of them.

The NFF, however, did not like my new friends at Betsson. Norsk Tipping – the Norwegian lottery organisation – is their main partner, so Norwegian players have to steer clear of all other betting firms, they believe. Or should I say, the association demands it. Since I didn't play in Norway or for the national team any longer, they couldn't do anything about it.

The same day the agreement was announced, the president of the NFF, Yngve Hallén, made a comment to the media. 'Disappointing and sad,' he said. 'An attack on the bedrock of Norwegian sport.' He was furious.

What Hallén and the NFF demanded of me was a loyalty that I felt they had never even come close to showing me. I was not willing to give them that. At least not while their arguments didn't hold water.

The NFF try to present it as though Norsk Tipping were practically some morally superior, idealistic organisation, but it's a betting company just like all others. Norsk Tipping profits enormously from the historic position the firm has in Norway. They have an exclusive arrangement with the NFF, and the good part of that agreement is obviously that it gives money to children's and grassroots football. The criticism by the association, levelled at players who advertise for a rival company after their career is over, is that we lack a sense of solidarity.

But on several occasions Betsson have expressed a desire to contribute to Norwegian sport, if they were allowed to compete under the same conditions as Norsk Tipping. The problem is that the NFF has profited nicely from Norsk Tipping for years, nurtured as they are within the Norwegian model.

'I believe this is an affront to what we stand for in Norway. Norsk Tipping is an important supporter of Norwegian sport, and what John Arne Riise is doing now, it is an attack on those who have contributed to his development,' Hallén said to *Dagbladet*.

Hallén made it sound like I hadn't been there for Norwegian football, for the children and for grassroots football. That's really disappointing. Let's for the moment disregard the fact that I played 110 internationals, never declined a single call-up, not even during the darker and more difficult periods of my life. And every time I was selected, I did everything the NFF asked of me: press interviews, adverts, football shoes for their kids. I've also tried to give back as much as possible. For example, for years I've arranged a summer football camp for 150 children between the ages of twelve and fifteen. One summer I even got Steven Gerrard to come along and teach them ball control, long passing and shooting. And since we had over four hundred kids on the waiting list, we made some short videos that were shown on TV2. I have been a Right to Play ambassador for many years, run a project called 'Riise Charity' and contributed tens of thousands of pounds in support of Médecins Sans Frontières and Save the Children. It's the least I could do. I don't think it's something I should brag about but I feel like the NFF has forced me to talk about it.

'Some individuals are more worried about their own wallets than about the people who have volunteered and been there during the building phase,' Hallén said to *VG*.

In addition there have been kit sales, billboards, sponsor dinners and appearances. The NFF does all of this to earn money off my name.

In return they've gone out of their way to distance themselves from me any time some media storm has blown up. My loyalty to Betsson is to do with the fact that I immediately got the sense that they believed in me, supported me and wanted to stand by me through thick and thin.

According to Hallén, I'm ungrateful for everything the NFF have done to further my career; that they've practically carried me on their backs.

'This is not the way to say thank you from someone who has benefitted from this,' he said.

Hallén has clearly forgotten that I left Norway at the age of seventeen. Incidentally, a transfer that provided my former club with millions. I still remember what the NFF said to the media back then. I remember reading the article right before I boarded the plane. They said that I wasn't ready. They said that decision would put a brutal end to my career.

71

WHEN DOES A FOOTBALL CAREER END?

It's a well-established fact that goalkeepers can play top-level international football for an eternity. There's less wear and tear on their bodies. There are plenty of examples: Dino Zoff, Peter Shilton and Gianluigi Buffon. Attacking players often get moved down the pitch because over the years they lose some pace. I played in defence. Unlike central defenders, I liked to move up the wing to take part in the attack, but always made it back to defend the counterattack, week after week, year after year. I was a vigorous and tough player. I was on the giving and receiving end of plenty of collisions. As a professional footballer, I had to be physically prepared at all times. If not, I wouldn't be capable of tackling the mental pressure that goes with being evaluated in the full glare of publicity, match after match. My body and my mind had been through a lot over nearly twenty years. For me it wasn't chiefly the body that began to tire, it was the mind. I had considered retiring as far back as when I ended my time at Fulham, only to go to APOEL, which with all due respect must be considered a much smaller club than any of the four I'd previously represented outside of Norway. Subconsciously I think I was tempted by exactly that – I had started to get bored. A lot of people probably think I'm an idiot for saying that. I've lived the dream and had a privileged life, but I started to feel like I'd had enough of being a footballer. I wanted to fade into the crowd more, go underground a little. I didn't know how much longer I could manage to spend in the spotlight. The wear and tear felt worse than before. In a not-too-distant future I would be done, I knew it. A time would come when I no longer had it in me. That was a difficult and weighty admission but it was the truth. I just hadn't fully accepted it yet.

72

I DIDN'T SEE OUT MY CONTRACT IN CYPRUS. THE TEAM WERE FAR superior in the domestic league, and even though over 20,000 people came to the matches, it lacked a spark of excitement and unpredictability. We won the league and cup in my first season, I'd scored six goals and all things considered didn't feel like I had much more to prove when the summer of 2015 arrived. Cyprus was not exactly the liveliest place in the world, either. I'm from Ålesund, so I'm used to the quiet, but Louise is from Oslo. All the same, the victories and the goals at Cyprus had given me a feeling that I was back in business. I wanted to return to the spotlight. There was just one problem. There was no longer much interest in me. The offers were not exactly pouring in. My career was coming to an end, plain and simple. Obviously I realised that but didn't want it to happen. Now I was really flying again. Come on, one last foreign adventure?

One day that summer I got a text message. It was written half in English, half in Swedish. The man who sent it was president of an Indian club; his name was Prashant Agarwal and he was married to a Swede. They were going to start a professional league in the country, the Indian Super League. They hoped to attract as many big names as possible. He asked if we could meet. I replied yes, because it set in motion the idea of being part of something new. Few people get to experience a new culture like that. Anyway, the season would only last for three months and the salary was good. And – not least – one of my greatest defensive role models was going to coach the team: Roberto Carlos.

I met the Indian club president and a Swedish agent in a strange location across the border in Sweden. Louise and I drove there, to this desolate spot by a lake. At a restaurant there, he presented his plan. His team was called the Delhi Dynamos. He said that he regarded football as an instrument to accomplish change in his home country. Greater equality between the sexes, improved health services for the poor. He had suffered from lung cancer and had decided to devote his life to that cause. One of the reasons he wanted stars in the league was to give the children and young people of the city role models. Did I fancy being a part of that? Yes, sure. As we drove back through the woods, I remember thinking about my dad for the first time in a long while, the sight of him in the hospital bed, all skin and bones.

The contract was signed as a kind of marketing ploy at the Emirates Stadium in conjunction with an Arsenal-Liverpool match on 24 August 2015. Ian Rush presented me with my new jersey, which depicted the team logo of a lion.

Let me start with the positives: the people I met in India were really nice. Everyone did their best. I had a beautiful room at a five-star hotel. More than 20,000 people came to the matches, a lot of young people. I was voted the league's best defender.

But India also presented a number of challenges.

We'd played a match against Goa. One of the players on their team, a Frenchman called Grégory Arnolin, had argued with me through large parts of the match. He had punched me in the stomach when he went past me, that was how it all started. We threw shit back and forth at each other. But after the match I expected things – like they almost always do – to be forgotten. But when the teams had dinner together at a hotel afterwards, Grégory just kept at it. I told him to bring it on – I was right there if he wanted to do something. Now we were close to flying at each other, and Louise, small as she is, got between us: 'Hey, both of you get your acts together now,' she said separating us. Then Grégory looked at her in indignation: 'Did you touch me? Don't you dare touch me. You don't know what I'm capable of. I'm going to kill you for that.'

The Indian organisers were so embarrassed afterwards. They forced him to apologise to her.

Louise was used to having a lot going on. Here she had nothing to do.

And to be threatened suddenly like that was the final straw: she couldn't take any more.

After four or five weeks she went home. So I was alone again. There were two months of the contract remaining. I'm not very good at being alone to start with, but the most exciting part of my day was training in the morning. The pitch was a long way away, so every day began with us being driven an hour outside the city, then an hour back. Everything had to be done together. We ate at the hotel. The physical training took place at the hotel. The club didn't want us to do things on our own. So I sat in my room. I watched films. But often the internet wasn't working, so that was no good either. One hour drive, training, one hour drive, hotel. Day in and day out. Hour after hour. Minute after minute. I just sat there. In the end I barely felt like doing anything, either. I lost all desire to think of something to do, this from the guy who usually has ants in his pants. I sat staring at the wall. I realise now that I was probably depressed. At least heading towards depression. I just sat on a bed in a hotel room in Delhi for two months.

Finally I managed to leave for home, wherever home was now. Louise and I had first found a place to live in London, moved to Cyprus, lived in a flat in Oslo, then on to Delhi, but at this exact moment, home was Oslo. Or, home was now with Louise. I didn't want to be alone again. According to the contract with Delhi Dynamos I was obliged to play the following season as well but I said that it wasn't going to happen. It wasn't going to work.

I had to find my calm again. We had moved from London in the summer of 2014. I had played one year in Cyprus, then been without a club for half a year, before playing three months in India. At the latter two clubs, I had requested that the contracts be cancelled early. I was 35. A football career rarely lasts much longer than that. I could see the end, I was prepared, but it was still a gloomy thought. I didn't feel like I was finished yet. I was not ready. I believed I had five years of top-tier football in me if I returned home. But more importantly than getting a few extra years in the sport that had given me so much prosperity and happiness, I wanted to go home. Even after all these years, even though I had left as a teenager, even with all the difficult things that had happened, with the city that certainly hadn't always wished me the best, home was still Ålesund. That was where I was from. I thought of the return as a kind of reconciliation. It was time now. I was going home.

73

THIS WAS THE SIXTH MOVE LOUISE AND I MADE IN LESS THAN FOUR
years. We still had three containers of belongings at a storage space in Oslo. I wanted
to conclude my career at Aalesund. There were a number of reasons. Everything
started there, obviously. Now there was even a statue of me outside the stadium, so
why not, right? I also wanted to play with my brother again, so that we were together
to the last, so to speak. We had shared a childhood and a dream. We had worked
hard for all those years. Playing with him would be the perfect conclusion. But more
importantly: Ariana lived in Ålesund with her mother. I wanted to connect better
with my first-born daughter.

As soon as rumours started to spread, the NFF smelt blood. For nearly three years
they'd had to sit and watch me screwing around for Betsson. Now was their chance
to put the breaks on. No player in Norway's top flight, Tippeligaen, could be paid by
a competing betting firm, they said. I had to annul the contract. Otherwise I could
just forget all about my grand plans of returning home.

I didn't know what to do. I so badly wanted to return to my daughter, my brother
and everything else. Yes, I could terminate the agreement with Betsson. But Betsson
had believed in me and backed me when no others would. It felt disloyal and bad
form to be forced to drop them. And I didn't want the NFF to win. Not after what
Hallén had said.

For me it was either Aalesund or retire. Things couldn't just fizzle out like this.
I tried to talk to the association, but the secretary general, Kjetil Siem refused to give
even one inch. He simply said no. At one point I was at Flesland Airport in Bergen,
when my phone beeped. It was a text message from Siem. No text. Just three emojis:
three pigs. I don't know what he meant by it but assume that it was not meant
as a compliment.

The matter was getting urgent if I was going to play in the league opener. On the night of Tuesday 8 March 2016, I posted a statement on Betsson's home page. The ties were cut. The arrangement was terminated. The adverts which had already been produced, another bone of contention with the association, would not be aired.

Betsson suggested it. They knew how much it meant to me to play in Norway. So they proposed that we terminate the arrangement until further notice so that I could make it work. Not only that, they said that the wages I would have received from them during this period would be accumulated, and that I would be paid retroactively when I stopped playing and started back at Betsson.

I was really touched.

Eleven days later – 19 March – I played for Aalesund's first team again; my last match for them had been when I was seventeen. Eighteen years had passed. It didn't go exactly as planned. I started on the bench in the league opener against Haugesund, which we lost 3–0. The same went for the first home match, another loss, this time against Brann. Against Rosenborg – where we lost our third match in a row – I started the match but was later substituted. In the next home match I played the full ninety minutes but again we lost. Well, I could go on like this but you can see where it's headed. I didn't play well. I was brought on, I was substituted. After thirteen matches I gave in. The motivation was no longer there. My head was tired.

I was done.

I no longer had it in me. The realisation hit me, there was no point in denying it any longer, and it was heavier and more painful than I had imagined. But time had passed, things were not exactly the same as before. I scored one goal. Not a particularly glorious or spectacular one, either. We struggled against the third division club Brattvåg in the third round of the Norwegian FA Cup: 0–0 after full time, 1–1 after extra time, then penalties. I took number two. It was the only goal of my comeback at Aalesund, a penalty against a team that averages 153 spectators at their matches, rather different than 100,000 at Camp Nou. And as if that wasn't enough: Brattvåg won the match.

74

'READY?'

'Yes, but I don't have as much time today. Louise and I are going on a booze cruise.'

'In the Porsche Cayenne that's outside?'

'Yeah, we've attached a roof box to the roof.'

'How's the new life, anyway?'

'I like it. Of course I wondered what it was going to be like. All my life I've played for a crowd. I've been able to feel their love and I didn't know what it would be like without that in my life. But it's been good. I was kind of prepared for it. My career was trailing off. I feel good. My eldest daughter is staying with us for a while. I'm helping her study for her exams. It feels good.'

'…'

'I flipped through the photo album of my dad and me the other day. I don't know why I did it. All of this has got me thinking about things.'

'Does it feel good?'

'Yes, well no, actually. It's almost like it gets more painful every time. The loss just grows bigger and bigger, it feels like. I wish …'

'What?'

'I think I'm going to get that tattoo.'

'Add his name?'

'Yes. And find his grave. Louise keeps saying we should do it.'

'Maybe she's right?'

'She usually is. She wants us to sit down and try to find it together.'

'…'

'Maybe I should give Nikola a ring, too, just to hear how things are with him.'

'Do you think you miss football, too? Maybe it increases the feeling of loss?'

'I don't know. As a player I've got nothing left to prove. There's nothing I haven't done. I've won the Champions League, I've played in front of 100,000 people. I scored all those goals when I was a child: to get on the district youth teams, get on Aalesund's first team, to then turn pro as a teenager and make the team after only two weeks, score game-changing, spectacular goals, play match after match, train hard and always go at it full throttle. I've achieved all of my ambitions. I can think back on everything that has happened. And only now when the stillness has settled in, do I realise what I couldn't understand then: I have succeeded in everything.'

'Still, don't you miss hearing a packed Anfield singing your song?'

'No. They still sing it. I can just go there if I want to hear it.'

'John Arne Riise ... I wanna know-ow-ow ... how you scored that goal ...'

'...'

'...'

'I won't be forgotten.'

75

I'M STANDING BY MYSELF ON THE PAVEMENT IN ÅLESUND CITY centre. On the other side of the street I see a young man I recognise. He's grown up now, like me, but he hasn't changed. It's one of the bullies from school. I follow him with my gaze. He's wearing some kind of uniform and at first I can't recall where I've seen that uniform before, but then I remember. McDonald's. Now I found myself walking after him. Tailing him almost, being careful to keep a safe distance. He slipped inside the McDonald's. I stayed outside for a while, then I went in. I knew what I had to do now. I stood for a moment watching him behind the counter. Then I joined the queue for his till. The whole time I stood there I made sure he didn't get away from me. If he swapped registers, I'd swap queues.

He served the family ahead of me.

Then it was my turn.

He routinely moved a tray in front of me and put a McDonald's placemat on top. 'How can I help you?' He looked up. I could see his eyes widen.

I ordered a meal deal.

'Just a moment,' was all he said after he had taken my payment. He found a paper bag, grabbed a burger, fries and soft drink and put everything in the bag. Then he gently placed it on the counter between us. I looked him in the eyes and smiled, then nodded briefly and picked up the bag. I felt its weight in my hand as I turned towards the door without a word. Calm and collected, I walked out to the street. All of Ålesund was bathed in sunshine.

Career

1997

- Called up for Aalesunds FK's first team at the age of sixteen.
- Nutmeg the team's biggest star at my first training session.
- I play nine matches for Aalesund, scoring one goal.
- Receive a call-up to Norway's Under-16s and Under 17s and proceed to score two goals in five appearances.

1998–1999

- I play in seventeen matches for Aalesund in the spring season, scoring four goals.
- Later that summer I sign for Monaco, having performed well for Norway Under-18s at the Nordic Championships. I play alongside French World-Cup winning stars Fabien Barthéz, Thierry Henry and David Trezeguet, and become a favourite of Jean Tigana, a legendary footballer himself. Monaco finish fourth in Ligue 1.

1999–2000

- I play 22 matches for Monaco in this campaign, and score my first goal for the club, a screamer from 40 yards.
- We win the league, finishing seven points ahead of our closest challengers Paris Saint-Germain.
- I make my debut for the men's national team and score my first goal.

2000–2001

- Monaco win Trophée des Champions, but I fall out of favour with the new manager. I still manage three goals in twenty matches amid much transfer speculation.
- At the end of the season I sign for Liverpool.

2001–2002

- At Liverpool we immediately win the Charity Shield and the UEFA Super Cup in the lead-up to my first full season, and I score my first goal for the club in the latter.
- Later I score against both Everton and Manchester United as we finish second in the league and reach the quarter-finals of the Champions League. In total I register eight goals in 56 matches.
- Match magazine select me as the season's best newcomer ahead of Ruud van Nistelrooy, among others.

2002–2003

- Liverpool win the League Cup, and I score six goals in 56 matches.

2003-2004

- A more difficult season, as Liverpool finish fourth and fail to capture a trophy. I also fail to get on the scoresheet in 35 matches.
- Still, I receive the Golden Watch for playing 25 internationals.

2004–2005

- Under Rafael Benítez we win the Champions League with Liverpool in a game dubbed 'The Miracle of Istanbul', after we come from three goals behind against AC Milan. I assist the first goal in the comeback, scored by Steven Gerrard. Over a million people greet us when we arrive back in Liverpool the next day.
- I score eight goals in 57 appearances in this campaign.

2005–2006

- We start the season by winning the UEFA Super Cup again, and I extend my contract with the club, committing until the 2008/2009 season.
- We win the FA Cup after another 3-3 draw in a final, this time against West Ham, and I score a penalty in the shoot-out. We finish third in the league. I play 52 matches and score four goals.
- I win the Kniksen Award in 2006, which recognises Norway's best footballer of the year.

2006–2007

- I reach my second Champions League final with Liverpool, having scored against Barcelona at Camp Nou in the Round of 16, the only professional goal I ever scored with my right foot. This time we lose to Milan, 2-1.
- We finish third in the league again, and I score five goals in 48 matches.

2007–2008

- In what turns out to be my final season at Liverpool I make 44 appearances, failing to get on the scoresheet.
- We reach the semi-finals of the Champions League and face Chelsea once more, and I score an own goal in injury time in front of the Kop. The goal proves decisive as Liverpool fail to reach a third final in four years.
- We still qualify for the Champions League after finishing fourth, but I am sold to AS Roma.

2008–2009

- I play 48 matches in my debut season in Rome – an amount beaten by only two others – and I score my first goal against Inter.
- I also get on the scoresheet against AC Milan in the San Siro with a thunderous free-kick in Paolo Maldini's last ever match.

2009–2010

- Roma challenge for a first league title since 2001, but in the end we have to settle for second place.
- I score a winner in injury time against Juventus, and Roma legend Francesco Totti describes me as 'a force of nature'. I have now scored in away matches against all three of the big Italian clubs: Inter, AC Milan and Juventus.
- I play more matches than anyone else – 52 – and score eight goals. Manager Claudio Ranieri describes me as the best left-back in Europe.

2010–2011
- Once again I am one of the team's mainstays, but Roma slip to sixth in Serie A.
- I move to Fulham to play alongside my brother Bjørn Helge Riise.
- Ninety-percent of readers select me at left-back when the Liverpool Echo names Liverpool's team of the decade.

2011–2012
- I become the national team's most-capped men's player ever, overtaking Thorbjørn Svenssen.
- I play 43 matches for Fulham as we finish ninth in the Premier League.

2012–2013
- I play 32 matches for Fulham as we finish twelfth in the Premier League.
- I retire from the national team with 110 caps to my name, a record still not beaten by anyone else in Norway, having scored sixteen goals.

2013–2014
- I play 25 matches for Fulham, returning to the team mid-season after being frozen out by Martin Jol.
- The team is relegated from the Premier League and so I move to APOEL Nicosia, a Cypriot team who qualify to play for the Champions League.

2014–2015
- I assist two goals on my debut and we win the Cypriot league and cup double in my first campaign. I score six goals.
- I play for the Delhi Dynamos in the inaugural Indian Super League season, and am voted the league's best defender.

2016

- After all these years I rejoin my first club Aalesunds FK, where my brother is playing.
- The comeback does not go as planned. After just three months and thirteen matches, it's over.
- I return to the ISL with Chennaiyin FC, playing ten matches before I retire from top-tier football.

2017

- I register as a player for SK Rollon, an Ålesund-based club in Norway's fourth division.

Acknowledgements

THE AUTHOR WOULD LIKE TO THANK THE FOLLOWING PEOPLE FOR advice, facts and information, various forms of contribution and input throughout the process: Susan Black, Stephen Done, Jonas Forsang, Steven Gerrard, Anders Hornslien, Are Kalvø, Ane Kolberg, Lars Backe Madsen, Marcus Magee, Donald McRae, Mikael Mellqvist, Pål Chr. Møller, Alexander Opsal, Bjørnar Valdal, Mari Stanisic Waagaard, Arne Scheie, Vladimír Šmicer, Mattis Øybø and Richard Aarø.

www.decoubertin.co.uk